SCUDAMORE'S
YEAR

SCUDAMORE'S YEAR
The National Hunt Season
1988–89

ALAN LEE

STANLEY PAUL

London   Sydney   Auckland   Johannesburg

Stanley Paul & Co. Ltd

An imprint of Century Hutchinson Ltd
62–65 Chandos Place, London WC2N 4NW

Century Hutchinson Australia Pty Ltd
20 Alfred Street, Milsons Point, Sydney 2061

Century Hutchinson New Zealand Limited
PO Box 40-086, Glenfield, Auckland 10

Century Hutchinson South Africa (Pty) Ltd
PO Box 337, Bergvlei 2012, South Africa

First published 1989
© Alan Lee 1989

Set in Linotron Bembo by
Rowland Phototypesetting Ltd
Bury St Edmunds, Suffolk
Printed and bound in Great Britain by
Butler and Tanner Ltd
Frome, Somerset

British Library Cataloguing in Publication Data

Lee, Alan, *1954–*
    The greatest hunt on record:
    the National Hunt year 1988/9.
    1. Great Britain. National Hunt racing
    I. Title
    798.4′5′0941

ISBN 0 09 174184 X

PHOTOGRAPHIC ACKNOWLEDGEMENT

For permission to reproduce copyright photographs, the author and publishers would like to thank the following: AllSport, pp. 8, 10, 16/17, 19, 20, 21, 33, 82 (both), 83, 84, 92/93, 102, 104/105, 107 (both), 109, 112, 114, 115; ASP, p. 38; Ed Byrne, p. 62; City Syndication, p. 60 (right); Gerry Cranham, p. 60 (left); Tony Edenden, p. 59 (bottom); Stephen Markeson/*The Times*, pp. 64, 66/67; Bernard Parkin, pp. 11, 12/13, 14 (both), 15, 28, 30, 40, 41, 42, 43, 44, 45, 46, 47, 48, 49, 50, 51, 52, 53, 54, 55, 56, 57, 71, 73, 75, 76/77, 78, 86, 87, 88/89, 90, 91, 94, 95, 96, 97, 98 (both), 99, 100, 101 (both); *Racing Post*, pp. 18, 22, 25, 26, 27 (both), 37, 58, 59 (top), 61, 63, 69; George Selwyn, pp. iii, 35 (both); Colin Turner, pp. 80/81, 108, 111, 113, 116, 117 (both), 118/119, 120, 121.

CONTENTS

Foreword

If someone had told me at the start of last season that I was about to ride more than 200 winners I would have said it was utterly out of the question. I might have added that the bearer of this wild forecast should have his head examined. In fact, nobody did come up with such a prediction, precisely because history suggested it was not possible – but plenty did in mid-season, by which time I had already ridden the first 100. I continued to scoff at the notion, and with feeling.

It will probably only sink into my conscious mind in years to come, when things are not going so well, when injuries are niggling, horses are running badly and I am gloomily wondering where the next winner will come from. For all of us jump jockeys, there are plenty of times like that, and it is then that I will look back on the 1988–89 season with fond nostalgia and downright amazement.

In examining the background to my own record-breaking year, I will acknowledge considerable good fortune with the weather, which cost us only ten meetings, and with my fitness. Such factors, however, pale into insignificance next to the man who made the dreams come alive. For, if my seasonal figure of winners was an eye-opener, Martin Pipe's new record of training 208 winners is, frankly, quite unbelievable.

As I was on board 158 of that number, more than seventy-five per cent of my total winners, I probably know more about Martin than most and I have no hesitation in calling him the most thorough, innovative and committed trainer I have ever had the privilege to meet. I have found it constantly irritating that so many people have trumped up fanciful ways to knock him, but then I know this is an unfortunate trait in British sport – if someone proves himself outstandingly talented, there seems to be a strange compulsion to put him down.

Martin, I suspect, takes it all in his stride. Why should he worry, after all, when he trained more than twice as many winners as anyone else? Arthur Stephenson, who goes about his job in a similarly dedicated, undemonstrative and private way up in the north, had a marvellous season with 90 winners, yet he hardly rated a media mention amid the justified ballyhoo over Martin's feats.

Whether either of us can touch such heights again is, of course, open to enormous doubt. The same happy set of circumstances may never coincide again. But if they don't, we have at least done what we both thought was impossible.

What I have no doubt in saying is that the Desert Orchid story will run and run. For, while a certain jockey and trainer were creating new records, this spectacular, front-running grey was capturing the hearts and affections of the public in a way no horse has ever done during my career. Every time he ran, huge crowds turned up to cheer and, after several of his memorable wins, I joined an exodus from the weighing-room of admiring, often emotional jockeys who just wanted to applaud him in. I have never known that happen before and I don't suppose I shall ever see it again. The horse is a complete one-off and when he won the Cheltenham Gold Cup, against heavy odds, even those of us who rode against him were secretly pleased.

I suppose that we three characters, two men and a horse, are destined to dominate any analysis of the season past. For myself, however, I shall remember it as the season which elevated National Hunt racing to the front pages, as well as the back; the season in which our sport featured more than once on television's national evening news programmes, and the season in which public enthusiasm for jumping was swept to peaks I have not known before. It was, above all else, a phenomenal year for all who love jump racing and I shall always be grateful for it.

PETER SCUDAMORE

Being a champion jockey, even one of such phenomenal achievements, involves very much more than simply turning up at the races, getting aboard the horses and steering them home. Most days for Peter Scudamore begin like this – on the gallops at an ungodly hour with a horse which may be unfriendly, uncooperative or simply untalented. Often, the weather is cold, wet, windy or all three; sometimes, inevitably, even Scudamore would silently wish to be elsewhere

CHAPTER ONE

Peter Scudamore

O F ALL THE TRIBUTES heaped upon Peter Scudamore during his season of endless success, none were more illuminating than the words of Steve Cauthen and Pat Eddery.

For some years now, the genial American and the determinedly private Irishman have crossed swords at the head of British Flat racing. Each would expect about 800 rides a season and would hope for a strike rate of around twenty per cent winners. Neither, however, has yet touched the magical 200 – and this is on the Flat, where rides for the stars are more plentiful, the weather more amenable, injuries less likely and transport infinitely more agreeable.

Both men were staggered by the achievements of Scudamore and were gracious enough to say so. On Whitbread Gold Cup day, less than 48 hours after the double-century had been chalked up on one of many emotional occasions produced by this season, Cauthen made a presentation to Scudamore on behalf of all the Flat jockeys. It was a moment to treasure, the often prickly borders between the branches of this sport being breached by a genuine gesture of acclaim. It meant a lot to Scudamore. It would have meant equally as much to him to hear the bewilderment of Eddery as he discussed the matter.

'I have passed 200 in a season if you take Europe and Ireland into account,' explained Eddery. 'But I've never done it in Britain, and it isn't for the want of trying. For a National Hunt jockey to ride 200 is just unbelievable. I can fly to most meetings, I wouldn't expect too many falls and nor would I be constantly scared of good rides breaking down.' He shook his head decisively. 'I would have been confident it could never be done over jumps.'

So how did he do it? Many thousands of words have been written extolling the intense dedication of the champion; many more have acknowledged his uniquely successful relationship with trainer Martin Pipe. Credit for the all-conquering season lies somewhere between the two, but to even approach a position where the idea was feasible required a talent partly inbred, partly taught but largely learned and honed over years of critical self-appraisal.

'Scu', as he is known throughout the sport, is a perfectionist. He puts demands on himself from which other, only slightly less motivated riders, would shrink. He analyses his own riding with dispassionate depth and is far quicker to admit to mistakes than to indulge in smug, self-satisfaction. His energy is boundless and, if his features sometimes wear the gaunt appearance of one who is pushing himself to the limit, he is doing so because he wants to, because he loves the life and, pertinently, has an addiction to success. He has often said that he would go on riding for as long as the winners continued to flow and it is no throwaway line; Peter Scudamore has reached the stage where he needs success. If for

. . . and most of Scudamore's days end like this, poring over the five-day entries in the racing press, marking off likely rides and spending untold hours and uncounted sums on the telephone to owners and trainers. There are no rigid hours to the life of the jump jockey and for one as professional and committed as Scudamore, the words 'off duty' hardly exist during the ten-month season

Social commitments are an integral part of the duties of being a high-profile champion. Probably not all such engagements are as pleasurable as this one. It is 12 November 1988 and Scudamore receives a statuette and a framed photograph to commemorate winning the previous season's jockey's title. The event is the traditional Champion Jockeys' Ball at which the reigning champion always makes a speech. If Scudamore is slightly less adept at this than he is at riding winners, why should he mind? By the time these presentations were made he had already ridden an extraordinary 67 winners in the new season and his hat-trick at Cheltenham that very afternoon had included the Mackeson Gold Cup on Pegwell Bay

Although Martin Pipe and Charlie Brooks, his two main stables, kept him so well provided with rides that he hardly had to look elsewhere, Scudamore was always alert to the possibility of quality outside mounts becoming available. Cala paez, the vastly improved staying hurdler trained by Brooke Sanders, was one such horse

Tarconey was another fancied outside ride for Scudamore at the Cheltenham New Year meeting. Even when it seems so little is going wrong, however, this game can be a painful leveller; Scudamore, challenging with his usual timing and looking the likely winner, found his mount had other ideas – Tarconey ducked out past the last fence, crashing through the wing and depositing his distinguished passenger in an unseemly heap. The damage, thankfully, was nothing that gritted teeth and a hot bath could not put right

It isn't quite like Dad coming back from a hard day at the office, but they are pleased to see him safe and sound nonetheless. Peter is escorted back to the Cheltenham weighing-room after a fall by his wife Marilyn and sons Thomas (left) and Michael, both increasingly keen racegoers

One of the champion's very few regrets about the 1988–89 season is that he failed to ride a winner for his father, Michael, who trains a small string in rural Herefordshire. Michael, however, was frequently a highly interested spectator and here he shares a joke with his son and Martin Pipe at Chepstow on 27 December. The smiles were well merited – the Pipe–Scudamore machine churned out four more winners that day, including the Welsh Grand National with Bonanza Boy

any unforeseen reason circumstances were to change and his name begin to slip down the list of leading jockeys, I suspect he would rapidly divert his formidable ambition elsewhere.

We may be confident that this moment is some way off. Even in the exhausted aftermath of his *tour de force*, Scudamore was talking in terms of riding for another five seasons. It is likely he will eventually turn to training, as his father did before him, but in the meantime we should savour the unique presence of a man who has elevated the profile of the jump jockey in a way that no-one, not even the charismatic John Francome or the legendary Fred Winter, had managed previously.

There are of course close links between Scudamore and these two greats of an earlier era. It was Winter who lured him away from his commitment to David Nicholson for what Scudamore described as 'the best job in racing'. That it did not quite fulfil expectations was due, tragically, to the stroke suffered by Winter, interrupting and finally terminating his wonderful training career. With his yard passing into the care of the young and talented Charlie Brooks, however, Scudamore maintained the profitable association.

And then there is Francome. Whether he would concede the

Novice chases can be a nightmare for jockeys if either their own horse, or the opposition, is reckless at the obstacles. Scudamore, however, rode a high proportion of his winners in these fencing nurseries and Canford Palm, for Charlie Brooks, was his fifteenth of the season when he won at Kempton Park in early November. Here, the same horse is spectacular in defeat during a competitive novice chase at Leicester

Haydock Park was a favourite venue for both Scudamore and Pipe. On 14 December they arrived there for a two-day meeting with Scudamore on 94 winners. Beyond belief, the necessary six were all ridden at the meeting, and all trained by Pipe. When Fu's Lady (pictured) won the Boston Pit Handicap Chase the tiny winner's enclosure was a chaotic scrum of photographers, journalists and well-wishers. It was a pattern we were to see repeated at various stages of the record-shattering season though, on this occasion, it turned out to be premature. The disqualification of an early-season winner, Norman Invader, for failing a routine dope test, meant that Scudamore's 100th winner was later officially altered to Sayfars Lad at Ludlow, five days later. Needless to say, the trainer was M. C. Pipe

point or not, I fancy Francome has been the greatest influence over Scudamore. Not in style of riding, and certainly not in dress, demeanour or personality, but in giving him the incentive to win and to go on winning. Francome was champion jockey seven times, the sequence overlapping with Scudamore's increasingly desperate attempts to unseat him. It seemed he had succeeded in 1982 when he set up a commanding lead in the jockeys' championship, only for an injury, five weeks from the end, to give Francome the chance to close. Showing a dedication which few expected, Francome chased up and down the country, rode sufficient winners to draw level with Scudamore and then, as a startling gesture, called it a day in order that the title should be shared.

That episode, I believe, had a profound effect on Scudamore. While he appreciated the sportsmanship of Francome's withdrawal, he now wanted more than ever to be in the number one position as of right. He had to wait a while; indeed, he had to wait until Francome retired in the spring of 1985, with his seventh title in the bag. Then, no longer able to wrest the crown from him in a duel, Scudamore determined that he would win more races, and more titles than Francome had done. It was not something he publicly vowed, for he is not that type of person, but unwittingly it has spurred him on these past few years.

Soon, it was plain that Jonjo O'Neill's all-time record would be smashed. The media pressure became relentless but Scudamore, remaining cool, went south to Fontwell Park on 6 February needing three winners for the magical 150. He won the selling hurdle on Pipe's Delkusha (pictured) and then drew level with a popular win on Charlie Brooks' young hurdler, Battalion. Brooks later said he was so excited because he thought that this was the record-breaker. Scudamore knew different

He has now been champion for four consecutive seasons. With the share taken into account, this means he needs three more titles to beat Francome. His furious pursuit of winners, however, means that he is within range of the all-time record career aggregate – held, of course, by Francome. Another injury-free season should see his place in history guaranteed.

There was history enough about the season just past. Scudamore rode the fastest ever 50 winners, the fastest 100, beat Jonjo O'Neill's record of 149 in a season, topped 200 for the first time and, for good measure, took his own career total past 1000. Every other week, it sometimes seemed, we were applauding yet another entry in the record books. Scudamore, not by nature a man who allows the world free sight of his inner feelings, was sometimes sufficiently swept up in the emotions of the moment to show animations foreign to his image.

The morning of Tuesday 7 February. Scudamore sits in his Gloucestershire cottage home, dressed in his Austin Reed Great Britain jockeys team uniform, and whiles away a rare idle minute in a day which was to become steadily more hectic

This is not to be wondered at when one considers the relentless scrutiny he was under from media of all descriptions. Television, radio and newspaper journalists formed a travelling band, reuniting at various stages of the season as another record loomed. His face, and even his voice, became familiar to watchers of the evening national news bulletins.

When the 200 was achieved on 28 April, ITN chartered a helicopter to take Scudamore, his wife Marilyn and his sons Thomas and Michael from the afternoon meeting at Hereford (where he drew a blank) to the night meeting at Towcester (where, incredibly, he rode four winners). *News at Ten* devoted several minutes to the story. Jump racing has never had such publicity and Scudamore, who had often felt frustrated by the public anonymity of his sport and its stars, was the catalyst for a sudden surge in household awareness.

It was, for Scudamore, a local meeting. Warwick provided him with two rides, both for Pipe. He only needed the first. Anti Matter romped away with a modest novice hurdle and the record was his

The celebration pictures went on for an age but this one meant more than most. Michael Scudamore, a courageous and successful jockey himself, never interferes with his son's career but he cares deeply about it. Out of picture, doubtless composing herself after another nervous ordeal, was Peter's mother Mary, who never really wanted him to ride and now can never bear to watch when he does

There is a story Scudamore is fond of relating which faithfully reflects his difficulty in emerging from Francome's shadow. He attended a function, peopled by celebrities from various walks of life, soon after winning the championship for the second time. On being introduced to a complete stranger and giving his name, the vague response was this: 'Scudamore? Oh yes, you're the jockey, aren't you. I thought you had long, curly hair.' After the events of the 1988–89 season, only someone who has been in a monastery or on a desert island could be excused such an error.

It began, fittingly, on day one – Saturday, 30 July, a mere eight weeks after his previous season had ended with a score of 132 winners. As ever, the new campaign began in holidaymaker territory at Newton Abbot and, as everyone expected, Pipe and Scudamore kicked off with an odds-on winner, Rahib, winning a handicap chase at 10/11.

On the second day of the meeting, Monday, 1 August, Benisa Ryder won a modest novice hurdle at 4/1. This, amazingly, was the longest-priced winner Scudamore was to ride for Pipe until Strands of Gold won the Hennessy Gold Cup at Newbury on Saturday, 26 November, almost four months later. Strands of Gold was Scudamore's 83rd winner of the season; 61 of them had been trained by Pipe, and 31 of these had been odds-on favourites.

The pattern was established. Pipe and Scudamore made a monopoly of the West Country meetings which dominate the early weeks of the season but, when the opposition became tougher and the pickings richer, their striking rate hardly faltered. Liadett, an American-bred three-year-old who started off by winning at Devon in September, was sent out by Pipe and ridden by Scudamore to win at each of the first three Cheltenham meetings.

By comparison, Scudamore was riding a mere handful of winners for Charlie Brooks, but there was nothing resentful about the jockey's continuing relationship with Winter's yard. Far from it. He continued to school the horses twice a week, and each Sunday there would be a series of telephone calls involving Brooks, Pipe and the jockey in order that clashes were kept to a minimum. 'People keep trying to set me against Martin Pipe,' mused Brooks, later in the season, 'but the arrangement works very amicably.'

Pipe and Brooks dominated most of Scudamore's time and talents but he was always on the lookout for likely winners elsewhere. Mercy Rimell was a great admirer of the champion and used him when available; so too did the canny Epsom trainer, Reg Akehurst. Scudamore's first big-race winner of the season; on Pegwell Bay in the Mackeson Gold Cup, was also an outside ride but it did not accrue from a chance offer, rather from the alertness and professionalism of the jockey. On hearing that Tim Forster's regular riders, Carl Llewellyn and Hywel Davies, were both injured and out of the big Cheltenham November meeting, Scudamore rapidly called the trainer on his mobile phone to offer his services. Offer accepted; good business all round.

To drive with Scudamore, to and from a meeting, is to know just a little more of what makes him tick. On the rare occasions when he has the luxury of the passenger seat (for him, there is only very seldom the convenience of a helicopter and never the private plane favoured by prominent Flat jockeys) the outward journey will be punctuated by rustling of the racing papers, delving into the formbook and frequent calls on the car phone. It is not a relaxed experience. Homeward, win or lose, he is a different man, chatting about the day and making fewer calls.

He is, however, never off duty and no sooner is he home each evening than phone messages have to be answered, the racing calendar studied anew and rides booked four and five days ahead. He likes eating and drinking but can do each only in strict moderation. If required on the morrow to ride at the minimum 10 stone, he will probably go without both.

The routine is undoubtedly punishing but you will hear precious few complaints. Unlike many of us, who return home cranky and complaining after a long and unproductive day, Scudamore will look forward to the next challenge with untapped relish. Sure, he broods if a big race has gone badly awry, but he is never so depressed as when he feels he has personally contributed to a horse's defeat. Then, as his wife will confirm, he can be insufferable. Gladly, such occasions were collector's items during this glorious winter.

Constantly seeking improvement in his style and his tactical grasp, Scudamore will study the video of a defeat more closely than a victory, searching for the instant in which the race may have eluded him. He has changed his opinions in various ways these past few years, and the association with Pipe has unarguably been responsible for him riding a high percentage of races from the front – dictating the pace, staying clear of trouble and maximizing his own horse's fitness which, in the case of virtually all Pipe's animals, is a formidable advantage.

Pipe provided him with victories in the Hennessy (Strands of Gold) and in the Welsh Grand National (Bonanza Boy). Both horses were thought of as potential Grand National winners and, indeed, Scudamore ended up riding Bonanza Boy at Aintree, as well as in the Cheltenham Gold Cup. On both occasions he was a gallant also-ran and these two races, the highlights of the jumping season, continue to evade him, continue to give him fresh incentives to chase.

Quite what else is left to him now, apart from pursuing Fran-

When the season began, few people outside jump racing would have recognized this face, no matter that he had been champion jockey for three successive years. Jockeys suffer anonymity through the nature of their job and its equipment but now, after more appearances on News at Ten *than many of our leading politicians, Peter Scudamore's face is recognized in many more households around the country*

come's record of longevity, it is difficult to imagine. Some of us, granted such a fantastic domination, would be content to sit back and look a shade scornfully upon the hapless pack. Not Scudamore. On Saturday, 27 May, a week before the end of the season, three jump meetings were scheduled. They were at Cartmel, in the Lake District, Hexham, in Northumberland, and Southwell, in rural Nottinghamshire. Three more rustic or remote meetings on the same day would be hard to invent, yet Scudamore contrived to ride at two of them, and was thwarted only narrowly in the notion of covering all three.

Anyone relying on the champion to rest on his laurels is suffering a dangerous delusion. If there is a more committed professional sportsman in Britain than Peter Scudamore, I have yet to meet him.

Here is the ultimate reason for public awareness. It came at Towcester, in rural Northamptonshire, on a late April evening. Dusk was falling when Scudamore went out on Gay Moore, a spare ride in a handicap chase. He came home alone, punching the air in recognition of winner number 200; his close jockey friend Hywel Davies was quickly alongside to congratulate him; then, composing himself yet grinning uncontrollably, it was back to the cameras and the champagne

CHAPTER TWO

Martin Pipe

A S ONE OF THE NATION'S CHRONIC PESSIMISTS, Martin Pipe will doubtless be shaking his head over what he might do for a job this time next year. After all, he trained 208 winners this past season. Things can only go downhill from there.

Pipe is the ultimate racing enigma, a mystery man whose journey from obscurity to previously unconquered peaks has aroused all manner of high emotions, not all of which have had anything to do with admiration. Michael Dickinson discovered in the early 1980s that exercising a monopoly may influence people but it does not necessarily make friends; Pipe, in eclipsing the prize-money record earned by Dickinson and elevating the training of winners to a level few had considered possible, has attracted jibes and jealousies from both inside and outside his profession.

It is hard to know whether Pipe is remotely concerned that his achievements must wait for the judgement of a future generation for their merit to be put into perspective. It is hard to know what he is thinking at any single moment. An intense, private man with no great desire to befriend or cultivate the media nor to make more frequent or fulsome public utterances than are strictly necessary, Pipe is also conspicuously not one of the crowd in his chosen job. Many trainers mix socially, on and off racecourses; Pipe prefers the company of his own team, which in itself breeds wholly unwarranted suspicion.

The best explanation for a phenomenon is often the simplest. In this case, it is that Pipe trains his horses harder, more thoroughly and with better facilities and back-up than any of his

The sun shone throughout the early weeks of the season and Martin Pipe made hay, setting an unprecedented pace with a relentless stream of winners at the early West Country meetings

It was at Newbury in late November, however, that anyone who continued to doubt his ability to train the big winners had to swallow their pride and own up. Pipe's achievement in producing Strands of Gold, first time out, to slaughter a competitive Hennessy Gold Cup field was perhaps the training feat of the season

rivals. He runs them only when they are bursting with fitness and only when he believes they have a winning chance. He uses the best jockey of modern times, who just happens to be on his professional wavelength. The extraordinary results of this elementary formula are there in print for all to see.

What can never be successfully argued is that Pipe has had a disproportionate number of the best horses. Indeed, that natural pessimism is never more pronounced than when discussing the virtues of his inmates. To listen to him, one could be pardoned for believing that eighty per cent of the horses in his yard were next to useless. There is, too, a strange logic in the assertion, for Pipe wins, and wins regularly, with horses of whom other trainers had despaired. He wreaks quite astonishing improvement from apparently modest animals and, combined with his shrewd placing of runners and the riding style of Peter Scudamore, transformation is often complete.

How he does it is privileged information but it is no secret that Pipe commits himself to his work with an intensity which is almost frightening. Training is hard work for all who do it properly, and let no-one say differently, but Pipe's life is so dominated, so obsessed by racing that it is a wonder he finds time to sleep. When he does, it seems a fair bet that his dreams are of only one subject.

He does permit himself a foreign holiday each year, though it is not the away-from-it-all paradise sought by most. He takes with him a heavy supply of form books and sales catalogues and, according to his staff, he phones the yard several times each day.

His annual telephone bill must be astronomical. Each evening, no matter whether they have been together at racing, he and Scudamore will have a telephone conference lasting anything up to two hours. They will discuss every aspect of their runners' performances that day before moving on to a detailed dissection of prospects for the following day. Their discussion will focus not only on the Pipe-trained horses but on the potential dangers and their style of running. Pipe says Scudamore has 'taught me so much about racing'. Scudamore might demur from such praise. He says Pipe is 'an absolute genius'.

Even on the gallops or at racing, Pipe is accompanied by the bleeping of his portable telephone. He hates being out of contact with his headquarters, and probably the only time he is uncontactable comes when he uses his own helicopter to travel to race meetings. In his Rolls-Royce, with the personalized MCP1 plates, a phone is always at hand.

Such trappings of success and wealth have undoubtedly been earned. Fifteen years ago, Pipe, then aged 30, was helping out in one of his father Dave's chain of bookmaking shops and riding –

A feature of the relationship between Pipe and Scudamore was their shared knowledge. Scudamore would pass on his views on every opposing horse, as well as every one of Pipe's, and the trainer would constantly be adding to the bottomless store of information at his disposal. Watch him in the parade ring before any race and he will be studying each horse as he walks around and noting his thoughts on his racecard

badly, in his unashamed opinion – in point-to-points. He rode only one winner and sustained the leg injury which still plainly troubles him now to a degree that he uses a bicycle to get around his yard rather than walk.

Encouraged by his father, he took out a permit to train a couple of family point-to-pointers under rules. On 9 May 1975 at his local Taunton meeting he sent out a horse called Hit Parade to win a novice hurdle. It was worth the princely sum of £272 but it was a winner which ensnared Pipe. He had the bug and he has never shaken it off, nor wanted to.

The following season brought five winners, a score he equalled the next year. By now, he held a full training licence but there were no indications of imminent stardom. In 1977–78 he trained only two winners. From that year on, however, the trend was rapidly upward, his score rising to six, twelve and, in 1980–81, fourteen, of which by far the most influential was Baron

Blakeney, who won the Triumph Hurdle at Cheltenham at 66/1 and brought the name of M. C. Pipe to a far wider audience.

By 1986–87 he was training 100 winners for the first time and only the foolish were prepared to dismiss it as a fluke. Although he ran down his own ability and his prospects with monotonous regularity, Pipe broke Dickinson's record of 120 winners in the 1987–88 season. Follow that, we thought – but he has done.

Along with a devoted and extensive team, in which the most prominent figures are his capable wife Carol, and his wise-cracking assistant Chester Barnes, Pipe not only added a staggering 79 winners onto his own record, and the little matter of £230,000 onto Dickinson's prize-money figure, he also proved he could win big or small events on virtually any course in the country.

It was symbolic that Pipe should win the very first event of the season, a novice chase at Newton Abbot; it seemed strange that he did not have a winner on the very last day, ten months later. Such was his domination. Between times, to his advantage, was such a mild winter that only twenty fixtures were lost to the weather. This not only helps a trainer in the obvious sense that there are more races than usual to win, but also in the uninterrupted preparation and planning of each horse's programme.

There were the prolific winners like Celcius, a modest middle-distance maiden on the Flat and by no means a straightforward ride. Most of the Pipe–Scudamore combinations could be seen setting off in front, setting a ferocious gallop to utilize their fitness advantage and making all to win. Not Celcius. He had to be held up until the last possible minute if he was to produce his turn of foot; he was also, in Pipe's words, no better than a selling-plater. Despite that, he had won three races by the end of August and went on to land nine in all, ranging from sellers to handicaps.

At the other end of the scale came the stable stars who were nursed to their targets: horses such as Beau Ranger, Corporal Clinger, Bonanza Boy and, perhaps most notably, Strands of Gold. This horse had joined Pipe from Jimmy Fitzgerald, that astute and highly successful northern trainer who is not accustomed to having good horses taken away. Pipe had something to follow here. He did it by producing the horse superbly fit first time out to win the Hennessy Gold Cup at Newbury by a comfortable six lengths. He was never right again after falling next time out at Ascot, and plans to run him in the Grand National, for which he would probably have started favourite, had to be scrapped. The Hennessy triumph, however, remained a quite brilliant example of training.

Corporal Clinger won the valuable Mecca Bookmakers Handicap Hurdle a week later and, just after Christmas, Pipe reached

The facilities at Martin Pipe's Somerset yard are one of the major reasons he has developed so quickly into a training star. Nothing is left to chance. Here, Pipe supervises some young inmates on the indoor horse-walk. Below, part of his 100-strong string walk to exercise

his fastest-ever century when Delkusha won at Taunton. The same horse was to carry him past his own winners' record six weeks later, in a week dominated by the trainer and his jockey. The following day at Warwick, Scudamore rode his 150th winner of the season, another new record – and, almost inevitably, it was gained on a Pipe-trained horse.

By now, further big-race winners had been earned. Bonanza Boy, whose ultimate target was the Cheltenham Gold Cup, had made a mockery of what appeared to be a competitive field for the Coral Welsh National on 27 December, a day when Pipe sent out no fewer than five winners. And at Haydock, on 21 January, Out of the Gloom stormed to victory in the Premier Long Distance Hurdle to give yet another indication of the Pipe magic.

Pipe had given Out of the Gloom a gentle reintroduction following a lengthy spell on the sick list. Running in a stayers' novice chase at Newton Abbot in early January, he had won with such authority that a prosperous career over fences seemed assured. Pipe put him back over hurdles at Haydock with similarly impressive results and Peter Scudamore had taken to thinking of him as his banker for the Cheltenham Festival, whichever race he was nominated to run in. Sadly, we shall never know if he was right, for in one of the few serious setbacks to cloud Pipe's season, Out of the Gloom died on the gallops one February morning. In jump racing, no matter what your rate of success, there is always something to bring you crashing back to earth.

As Cheltenham approached apace, with no hint of severe winter weather, Pipe remained constantly in the headlines. Haydock Park, the enterprisingly run Lancashire course which Pipe names as his favourite in the country, had come up with a scheme encouraging more runners in their steeplechases. They offered a £25,000 bonus to any yard scoring six winners from at least eighteen chase runners during their jumping season. Pipe, with an impatient disdain, did the difficult part with the first six horses he ran there over fences. The other twelve runners followed, some of them seeing fences for the first time, and a healthy cheque arrived in the Somerset village of Nicholashayne.

Cheltenham itself might so easily have been an anti-climax, but the very first race of the Festival ensured that it was not. Sondrio, unfancied for a Pipe horse at 25/1, won the Supreme Novices Hurdle – ridden by Jonathan Lower because Pipe had advised Scudamore he would be better off riding something else. The other novice hurdle, the Sun Alliance over 2½ miles, also went to Pipe through Sayfars Lad; again, Scudamore had elected to ride another horse. Such fallibility might have been infuriating for the jockey himself but, in a season of relentless domination, it was oddly comforting for those who could only look on admiringly.

The moment the impossible was suddenly a reality. The long and gruelling, yet ultimately rewarding season is well into its final month and Pipe hits the 200-winner mark with Anti Matter at Stratford's evening meeting on 19 May. Coincidentally, this was the same horse which gave Scudamore his record-breaking 150th winner

On 4 March, Pipe had trained six winners, spread across three meetings, and probably alerted the majority for the first time to the real possibility that he might crack the 200 mark. By mid-May, however, the trainer was still morosely discouraging whenever the subject arose. When Mighty Prince won a selling hurdle at Worcester on 16 May, the Pipe score climbed to 193. The trainer, conceding at last that the double-century was in reach, gave his view that if it was to be done at all, it would have to wait for an all-out assault on the Bank Holiday meetings of 29 May – coincidentally, his 44th birthday.

His present arrived early, for over the next three days he trained the necessary seven winners, climaxing with an emotional double at Stratford's evening meeting on 19 May. The backslapping never stopped and nor, for some while, did the champagne. I have seldom seen Pipe so relaxed – yet, a fortnight later, back on the same course, that mobile phone was bleeping and the familiar furrowed brow was working overtime. The current season had brought its records and its rewards; you could sense that Pipe had now turned his attention to next season, and new horizons.

CHAPTER THREE

Issues and Highlights

In the weeks before Desert Orchid began to monopolize the major steeplechases, three good prizes were claimed by the eight-year-old gelding Pegwell Bay. Trained in Oxfordshire by Captain Tim Forster, a man whose interest in hurdlers is strictly a means to a future over fences, Pegwell Bay had won three races the previous season, all over 2½ miles, and proved himself a rare specialist at this trip in the first half of the new campaign. Utterly game, and a quick, economical jumper, Pegwell Bay won first time out at Newbury under his regular partner Carl Llewellyn, a sensitive and improving young horseman. When Llewellyn was injured,

Captain Forster was briefly without a jockey for his tilt at the Mackeson Gold Cup . . . but only until the ever-alert Peter Scudamore heard of the vacancy and rang the trainer to offer his services. Scudamore teamed up successfully with Pegwell Bay to win the Mackeson (pictured) but, four weeks later, with Llewellyn still injured and another tempting 2½-mile race on offer back at Cheltenham, the champion deserted him to ride Martin Pipe's Beau Ranger. Brendan Powell came in for the spare and, in a thrilling finish, held on well to beat Beau Ranger by one-and-a-half lengths

The novelty of having a senior member of the royal family riding in a handicap chase has still not worn off with the race-going public. Nor should it. The essential adventurism of those involved in the sport, and the intimacy of those who merely look on, is encapsulated by HRH The Princess Royal striding to the parade ring alongside Scudamore, Sherwood and various 7-pound claimers for a minor event at, shall we say, Ludlow. The Princess, who rides with ever-increasing assurance and expertise thanks largely to the bi-weekly coaching of trainer David Nicholson, is pictured at Worcester in October aboard General Joy, bought for her to ride by the Save and Prosper Group. Sadly, after being in the frame in each of four previous runs, General Joy collapsed and died at Chepstow in December. The Princess, however, continued to ride her own horse, Canon Class, over fences and increased the pleasure of spectators and the takings of racecourses

When The Thinker won the Cheltenham Gold Cup in 1987, his trainer Arthur Stephenson was conspicuous by his absence. He had chosen to saddle a few runners at Hexham instead. Widespread astonishment resulted, but this was typical of a man who has never enjoyed the limelight, much less sought it. Stephenson is a gruff and deliberately unapproachable Bishop Auckland farmer, but his skill at preparing and placing his horses remains as potent as ever. He turned 69 years old this season, and also clocked up 30 years as a trainer but, despite the absence through injury of his stable jockey Chris Grant for four months, he ran more horses, and trained more winners than anyone except Martin Pipe. Many of the winners were gained on remote northern courses such as Sedgefield and Hexham, where he has no peer, but Stephenson is never scared to send a horse with ability to one of the rich southern meetings, even if he personally prefers to stay at home. Giolla Padraig, one such horse who made regular journeys south, is pictured winning an amateur riders' steeplechase at Cheltenham's October meeting

There are few more popular owners in National Hunt racing than Peter Hopkins, a genial Welshman who made a successful living in the schools travel business and then indulged his passion for jump racing to the full. Hopkins has most of his horses with his long-time friend and fellow cricket-lover, Josh Gifford. These include Abbreviation, a prolific winner on fast ground, the handicap hurdlers Persian Style and Johnstons Glory, and one of the most

exciting young horses in Britain in Green Willow. Having run only once the previous season, finishing a close second to subsequent Festival winner Vagador, Green Willow was something of a 'talking horse' this term. Gifford and Hopkins knew as much, but sensibly started him off quietly, with a facile win in a minor event at Wetherby. Then, in December, this big, rangy horse took on some of the year's best novices at Cheltenham and slaughtered

them, despite unseating jockey Peter Hobbs and bolting on the way to the start. He won another valuable event at Newbury and was marked down by many as a banker for the Sun Alliance Novices Hurdle at Cheltenham but, after a defeat by Calapaez which far from disgraced him, he could finish only fifth at the Festival. Any disappointment for Hopkins was assuaged by the thought of Green Willow going straight over fences in the new

season. He looks a natural, as
Bernard Parkin's picture illustrates.
Hopkins, now living in Ireland but
still with designs on the title of
champion National Hunt owner in
Britain, also had winners during the
season trained by Gerry Enright, Jeff
King and Jonjo O'Neill, each of
whom rode for him during their time
as jockeys. O'Neill gave Hopkins
his most eye-opening success of the
season with Vicario di Bray
(pictured), who looked to be taking

on more than he could handle when
meeting the champion hurdler
Celtic Shot, among others, in a
conditions race at Haydock. But he
put up a staggering display to win in
mischievous style, shaken up only
50 yards from the line by Mark
Dwyer. On the strength of this he
went off as one of the shortest-priced
favourites in the history of the Tote
Gold Trophy (formerly the
Schweppes) but could finish only
second

The horse which foiled the gamble on Vicario di Bray was the tough and versatile Grey Salute, pictured looking rightly pleased with himself in the Newbury winner's enclosure with jockey Richard Dunwoody, owner Tony Hayward and trainer John Jenkins. Grey Salute had already won over 2 miles on the Flat and, for good measure, he returned to the level and won the valuable Ladbroke Chester Cup in May. In a crowded year, he had also won a competitive handicap hurdle at Fontwell prior to his Newbury triumph, and run disappointingly when well backed for the Champion Hurdle

Richard Dunwoody's total of 671 rides was higher than even Scudamore but he found time, just before starting this hectic season, to marry his long-time girlfriend Carol. Guests at the ceremony included Charter Party, on whom Dunwoody won the 1988 Gold Cup, plus his lad and the trainer David Nicholson.

In the 1989–90 season, Dunwoody will continue to be retained by Nicholson but has also taken a second engagement with the former champion trainer Nicky Henderson. He will also ride Desert Orchid, following Simon Sherwood's retirement

Arab domination of Flat racing has long been a cause of resentful opposition, so the incursion of Sheikh Mohammed and his famous maroon and white colours into the far less rarefied world of jump racing caused considerable interest, not to mention alarm. His first horse, Kribensis, was trained by the otherwise exclusively Flat-race handler Michael Stoute to win the 1988 Daily Express Triumph Hurdle and, this past season, he led all ante-post markets for the Champion Hurdle right up to race day. His second horse, Highland Bud, was sent to a more traditional jumping trainer in David Nicholson, and was just as successful. In the weeks leading up to the Cheltenham Festival, the Sheikh owned the favourites for both the Champion and the Triumph. Neither eventually justified the support, though both were plainly unsuited by the softened ground. Kribensis, a grey in a season of greys though much darker in colour than both Desert Orchid and Grey Salute, won twice at Newbury before taking the Christmas Hurdle at Kempton but, although in front approaching the last, his unbeaten record was lost at Cheltenham. Highland Bud, pictured beating Enemy Action over the Cheltenham course in January, ran gamely in the Triumph but had to give best to the mudlark Ikdam. He was later sent to Doncaster Sales, clear indication that success had not encouraged the Sheikh to pursue and expand in National Hunt racing. Sighs of relief from the thousands of small-time, sporting owners who are the lifeblood of the jumping game

Among the larger-than-life characters of the season, none was more ubiquitous and few more controversial than Colin Tinkler Senior, boss of the Full Circle group. Full Circle were among the innovators in what has now become a mass outbreak of horses in club ownership – in other words, the club or company owns the horses, and members who join receive the involvement of regular runners and, if they are very lucky, a dividend at the end of each year. There was no disputing the success rate of Full Circle. Their horses, trained by Nigel Tinkler in Malton and ridden by a talented retained jockey in Graham McCourt, were prolific winners all over the country. What did raise eyebrows, and provoke caustic comment, was the fact that many of the wins were gained in selling hurdles and the successful horses, some of whom were plainly running beneath their capabilities, were invariably bought in at a substantial loss. To many observers, it made no economic sense at all, but the members, whose pleasure at winning was augmented by Colin Tinkler's private telephone service advising them how much they would be sensible to bet on the runners, seemed happy enough. Tinkler, an unmistakable figure with a theatrical voice and style, was also quite plainly in his element when it came to bidding at the many auctions, like the one pictured at Worcester

In any other year the achievements of Mark Dwyer, the quiet Irishman attached to the powerful Yorkshire yard of Jimmy Fitzgerald, would have demanded regular headlines. But this was Scudamore's year and, just as the current champion lived his early seasons in the shadow of John Francome, so Dwyer was confined to the foothills now while 'Scu' climbed every available mountain. He would easily have exceeded 100 winners for the first time but for an injury in mid February, when the Fitzgerald horses were at the peak of their form. A week earlier, the point had been proved when the game staying chaser Proud Pilgrim beat a high-class field in Ascot's Charterhouse Mercantile Chase. He is pictured duelling on the run-in with Josh Gifford's under-rated Ballyhane; Dwyer would not be denied and his finishing strength, allied to the style he has long possessed, make him a formidable rival

MACKESON

One of the consequences of the unusually mild winter was that the valets, who work as hard behind the scenes as anyone involved in the sport, went very short of days off. Being an indomitably hardy and cheerful breed, they did not complain. Robin Lord took his leave from the job, however, and his official retirement as a master valet, at Cheltenham on Mackeson day, was marked by a presentation from clerk of the course Philip Arkwright. Also in picture are top northern jockeys Phil Tuck and Mark Dwyer, and the valet to most leading southern jockeys John Buckingham (second left)

John Buckingham at work.
Everything looks clean enough here,
but on days when the mud is ankle
deep, the job is less inviting and
very much more time-consuming

Since the retirement of John Francome, Steve Smith Eccles has become the senior jump jockey and consequently assumed the number one peg in a very democratic weighing-room. Peter Scudamore, despite his eminence as champion jockey several times over, has to make do with the number two position until Eccles retires – which he is not planning to do just yet. Reading right to left, Smith Eccles, Scudamore, Hywel Davies and Richard Rowe discuss an evidently serious point in what can often become an extremely amusing environment

No-one has ever trained steeplechasers better than Fulke Walwyn. This is the opinion of many good judges in the jumping game and this year, at the grand old age of 78, Walwyn was proving the point again with the exciting stayer Ten Plus. A leading hurdler three years ago, Ten Plus took time to acclimatize to fences but, with Walwyn's patience and tuition behind him, he remained destined for stardom. Two comfortable wins at Wincanton and Chepstow early in the season convinced many people that here was a serious rival to Desert Orchid and the rest in the Gold Cup reckoning. Ten Plus returned from a break to win at Newbury on Tote Gold Trophy day and was heavily backed to give his veteran trainer a fifth Gold Cup. The tragedy of that day was momentarily obscured by the euphoria surrounding Desert Orchid's triumph, but it will remain etched in the memory of Kevin Mooney, Walwyn's stable jockey. Ten Plus was still in front, going well, when he fell at the third last fence, never to rise again. The fatality was too much for Mooney, a thoroughly likeable, workmanlike jockey who wanted nothing more than to give his loyal guv'nor the final triumph he craved. Mooney collapsed in tears on the weighing-room steps, quite the most emotional sight of the season

*On a far happier note . . . Mercy
Rimell, jockey Dermot Browne
and assistant trainer Johnny
McConachie are all smiles after Deep
Moment's surprise win in the
Charterhouse Chase at Cheltenham's
January meeting. At the end of the
season this trio all went their separate
ways: Mrs Rimell into reluctant
retirement; Browne to set up as a
trainer; and McConachie stepping
up to train under his own name at
Stratford-on-Avon, where a lot of
Mrs Rimell's former inmates would
be joining him*

One of the most successful
partnerships of the season was that
between Ross-on-Wye trainer John
Edwards and jockey Tom Morgan.
Although his stable star, Pearlyman,
missed the entire season through
injury, Edwards trained more
winners than anyone except Martin

Pipe and Arthur Stephenson in what
was emphatically his most successful
season. Yahoo, second in the Gold
Cup before winning at Aintree,
was the yard's flag-carrier but
Dixton House, a convincing
Festival winner and the beaten
favourite in the Grand National,

created enormous publicity. Dixton
House is pictured returning in triumph
at Cheltenham – a marvellous piece
of training by Edwards (right) to bring
the horse back so well after injury,
and further cause for bewilderment
that the stylish Morgan receives so
few outside rides

Plenty of people were ready to dismiss West Tip as yesterday's news when trainer Michael Oliver nominated him a definite runner for the Grand National again. But he ran so heroically in defeat at Aintree that the spirit was plainly still willing and he must have been one of the best bets of the season when cantering home at 9/4 in a hunter chase at Cheltenham later the same month. Marcus Armytage is in the saddle as he canters to post at Cheltenham. This may not be his final win, either, for Oliver is now keen for one final crack at the National in 1990

Desert Orchid is not the only grey who will hold a prominent place in Simon Sherwood's memory-bank. Knighton Lad (pictured) may never rise to the same dizzy heights but he gave Sherwood the last two milestones in an unforgettable season . . . his final winner on his

favourite Cheltenham course in April, and the last winner of his career at Haydock Park on May day. Sherwood, to many minds the closest in sheer style to Francome, had decided some time earlier that this would be his last season before following his brother Oliver into training. Naturally, he wanted to go out on a winner and as soon as Knighton Lad crossed the line at Haydock, he knew the time had come. In the past few years, Sherwood had become associated with a stream of high-class horses – David Elsworth's Desert Orchid and Barnbrook Again, plus his brother's The West Awake, to name perhaps the most notable three. He will be missed in the weighing-room for his humour and his style, but thankfully such qualities will not be totally lost to the sport

When the champion trainer and handler of the best-loved horse in racing finds himself threatened with the unthinkable loss of licence, the sport holds its breath. It was this way last December when, after ten months of exhaustive enquiries, David Elsworth appeared before the Jockey Club at Portman Square to answer allegations that he had administered steroids to his admirable staying chaser, Cavvies Clown. The horse had given positive dope tests after winning three races, at Newbury, Wincanton and Cheltenham, during January 1988; since then, the matter had hung like a guillotine over the affable, capable and extremely popular Elsworth.

He had subsequently won the Grand National with Rhyme 'n' Reason, along with numerous big prizes claimed by Desert Orchid. But success is no passport to immunity and, in the week of his 49th birthday, and the week when he received his Trainer of the Year award, Elsworth faced the music.

He was accompanied not only by his solicitor Jeremy Richardson (pictured, with glasses), but also by an analyst and a veterinary surgeon. As the Jockey Club had also assembled a high-powered team of experts, the hearing lasted a marathon seven hours. Then came the announcement that Elsworth had been found guilty both of administering the steroids and of misleading the stewards by denying that Cavvies Clown had received any veterinary treatment during the relevant period. He was fined £17,500, a record monetary punishment and one which meant he had not, after all, set a new prize-money record during the season in question. Elsworth, however, was allowed to retain his licence and that, after the grimness of the occasion receded, was an enormous relief to him

Barney Curley's familiar features are seldom far away from controversy. He and the stewards, it often seems, have been baiting each other for years and if the opinionated Irishman has sometimes come off painfully the worse from the exchanges, he has also enjoyed his moments of triumph. He battled successfully for the right to a trainer's licence and then showed he could use it by turning out sixteen winners in the 1987–88 season. He finished three short of that figure last season but continued to demonstrate skill with the placing and preparation of some notoriously bad-legged horses. He also spent more time in front of the stewards, though on this occasion it was in defence of his retained jockey, Declan Murphy, whose persistent whip offences brought him a swingeing suspension

Graham Bradley's relationship with the stewards and the racing public has never been better than turbulent. A supremely stylish horseman with what jockeys would term 'a clock in his head', the experienced Yorkshireman is nonetheless prone to monumental misjudgements which, on occasion, have endeared him to nobody. His season, and very nearly his career, was utterly spoiled by an extraordinary incident at Market Rasen in March when Starjestic, ridden by Bradley and trained by his father, Norman, went off at 5/4 favourite in a field of only three for a handicap chase. Bradley was unseated at the third last fence, the race going to Sidvic, and the local stewards referred the case to the Jockey Club. Lengthy investigations ensued before it was announced that Bradley would be called before an inquiry. It was fully two months after the race when Bradley was completely cleared of any impropriety, and by this time he had faced, none too good-humouredly, a torrent of abuse from punters when winning on the horse next time out. He had also lost his main riding job with David Murray-Smith and admitted: 'My credibility is pretty low.' At 28, however, Bradley has the talent to fight back. Next year will tell if he has the resolve and the confidence

Every jumping season brings its sadnesses and its tragedies. This one had more than most. Amid the euphoria which pursued Desert Orchid and the constant celebration which accompanied Pipe and Scudamore, there was heartache in the mere mention of three young and popular members of the jockey clan. Two of them died in early-season accidents; the other, a newly married girl, was permanently paralysed.

Vivian Kennedy (top left) was killed in action. He died from the effects of a fall at Huntingdon in August, having already persuaded some very good judges that he could be a new-generation star. He had

been attached to the Lambourn yard of Fred Winter, now taken over by Charlie Brooks.

The talent of Paul Croucher (top right) had already been established, with a regular supply of winners both for Kim Bailey and his retaining trainer, David Murray-Smith. Fresh-faced and ambitious, he was a hugely popular, unassuming member of Lambourn society, and racing plunged into a genuine grief when he was killed in a horrific late-night car accident.

For Jessica Charles-Jones (right), survival meant having to come to terms with the fact that she would never ride again. The daughter of West Country farming trainer

Bill Turner, Jessica had recently married another jump jockey, Gareth Charles-Jones, when her life was altered by a fall which left her semi-paralysed. Hospitalized for several months, she remained indomitably cheerful, complaining only of being bored, never of being victimized by circumstance. Brave in adversity as she was in the saddle, she is pictured shortly after her release from hospital. An appeal fund was set up in her name and racing, which has sometimes shown its disapproval of girl jockeys and the risks they encounter, donated wholeheartedly to one who would never have liked a sexual distinction drawn between jockeys

Michael Bowlby easily exceeded his previous best score with 28 winners at a healthy striking rate of nineteen per cent, but it was only in the closing weeks of the season that his name came to public prominence. He had registered one of the most impressive and convincing Cheltenham winners of the year on Nicky Henderson's Rustle at the March Festival, and in late April he gave another Henderson horse, Brown Windsor, an outstanding ride to land

the Whitbread Gold Cup on the rich Sandown Park mixed card. Brown Windsor was only a novice, owned in partnership by Bill Shand-Kydd and Michael Buckley, and it was the owners who persuaded Henderson he should take his chance in an event usually the reserve of seasoned handicappers. He is pictured jumping the last in the 3-mile 5-furlong marathon ahead of two distinguished victims, Gold Cup winner Charter Party and Grand

National winner West Tip. Soon after the celebrations came more good news for Bowlby, who is married to Jenny Pitman's sister Mandy. In the new season, he will ride as retained first jockey to one of the country's brightest young trainers, David Murray-Smith, a man who never wastes runs and whose rate of winners to runners this past season was bettered only by Martin Pipe himself

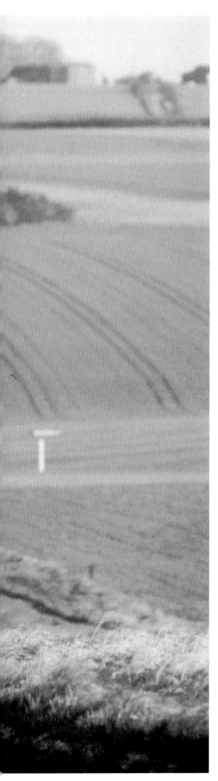

CHAPTER FOUR

Desert Orchid

T HE ROMANTIC ADVENTURE that is Desert Orchid's racing career had long since promised to develop into blockbuster proportions. He is, after all, the horse with every requirement for hero status – a vivid grey who jumps flamboyantly and demands to make the running. His record was formidable, with 21 wins over hurdles and fences when this season began. But if before he had been a welcome, colourful star, this was the year when he stole the entire show.

But for his startlingly uncharacteristic fall at Aintree in April, a lapse regarded by jockey Simon Sherwood as an indicator of seasonal fatigue, Desert Orchid would have gone through the 1988–89 campaign unbeaten. Moreover, the range of his six victories, from a 2-mile, fast-ground handicap at Ascot to the searching 3¼ miles of the Cheltenham Gold Cup in hock-deep mud, emphasized that here was not only the best steeplechaser in the country but also the most versatile.

As with all the best sporting stories, this one has many diverse and interesting strands to it. Few, presumably, have now escaped the probings of the varied documentaries, feature articles and books which the horse's exploits have prompted. They have gone into the ownership, fronted by television scriptwriter Richard Burridge; the work-riding of the unassuming Rodney Boult; the loving care and devotion of 'Dessie's' stable girl Janice Coyle; and, of course, the genius of trainer David Elsworth, a man as adept at turning out the winners of major races on the Flat as over obstacles. Then, there have been the jockeys – Colin Brown, who rode him to all his early wins and retired following the King

Previous page: *Rodney Boult, David Elsworth's head lad, on the Whitsbury gallops with Desert Orchid shortly before the Gold Cup. In the words of Elsworth: 'Rodney has played a major role in Desert Orchid's development. We argue like hell: he's always trying to underdo him because he feels sorry for him, and I'm not trying to overdo him, but Rodney thinks I am. But between us, we seem to get it just about right. Rodney would wrap him up in cotton wool and never do anything with him, whereas my concern is that unless we do our job right and get him to the races fit, we're not doing him justice. He's got a fairly big engine and he takes a lot of work, and if you don't get him 100 per cent fit he'll be found out on the racecourse, and it will hurt him there. Preparation is the most important thing, and Rodney knows as much about it as I do'*

Boult leading Desert Orchid back from the gallops, through the winding Whitsbury lanes. As he does on the racecourse, Desert Orchid always likes to be in front, and he will physically barge out of the way any other horse who tries to head up the string, even in the lanes

George VI Chase of 1987, and the sensitive, stylish Simon Sherwood, who had never experienced defeat on the spectacular grey until that fall at Liverpool.

Sherwood, too, has now retired, giving as he went a view that will meet few arguments in the racing game, namely that the jockey who takes over from him aboard Desert Orchid, now confirmed as Richard Dunwoody, will be the luckiest rider alive. He is not, as Sherwood never tired of saying, just another ride, nor even just another likely winner; he is the embodiment of all that is good about 'chasing, an exhilarating and utterly genuine horse who develops close and lasting relationships with everyone within his compass, from those who see and tend to him each day to those who simply turn up, in their adoring thousands, to cheer him as others would cheer a football team.

Make no mistake, the Desert Orchid fan club is real enough. Bizarre though it may seem for an animal to achieve such celebrity status, such massive public following, the enigma cannot be denied after the sights and sounds of this season past. Not since Red Rum has Britain so fallen for a steeplechaser – and, whereas 'Rummie' reserved his act for Aintree each year, Desert Orchid seems perfectly capable of turning on the style any day, and on any stage.

He had begun to kill off the myths about him a year earlier. His win at Liverpool, in April of 1988, was his first on a left-handed course and was achieved in such emphatic fashion, beating Kildimo by eight lengths, that the reservations many still harboured about him seemed obsolete. Still, however, he had not conquered Cheltenham; that would have to wait as Elsworth set him about his by now established pattern of races.

Wincanton was the starting point, just as it had been the previous season. As the crow flies, Wincanton is not far at all from the Elsworth stables in Whitsbury, near Salisbury, but in practice it is the sort of course which appears to be a very long way, and a very tough drive, from anywhere. Tucked away in a maze of country lanes north of the A303, it could give the passer-by the impression it was one of those rustic tracks peopled by farmers and raced upon by animals of dubious breeding and negligible ability. It is nothing of the sort. Wincanton, splendidly managed and enterprisingly progressive, is perhaps top of the second division as jumping courses go. Its prize money is good, its intelligent race-framing attracts the best horses from the top yards, and its crowds are often enormous. Sure, the local farming contingent is well represented, but so is the avid racegoer from all surrounding counties.

On 27 October they came in their thousands, for one reason only. Desert Orchid was back in business, having his first outing

Simon Sherwood suffered a mid-season injury which briefly put his participation in the King George VI Chase at Christmas in doubt. It was not a ride he was about to sacrifice lightly, however, and just before Christmas he was pounding around the lanes of his native Lambourn to prove his fitness

since beating Kildimo in a memorable battle for the Whitbread Gold Cup back in April. The Whitbread was a highly competitive handicap run over 3 miles 5 furlongs on the demanding Sandown Park course; the Terry Biddlecombe Chase did not present the same problems. A mile shorter, it might also have been framed specifically for Desert Orchid, so well did the conditions suit him. This, inevitably, resulted in a shortage of runners and a rather one-sided betting market, two factors usually designed to shrink a crowd. This, however, is where Desert Orchid breaks all accepted conventions. The crowds do not come to bet on him nor, necessarily, in the hope that he will have a hard race. They come because they want to see him; it is as simple as that, as unusual as that.

The phenomenon took shape at Wincanton, and a pattern was formed for the rest of the season. As Desert Orchid was saddled in the open-fronted boxes away to the side of the parade ring, a scrum of spectators formed to gaze at him. They followed, Pied Piper style, as he was led, his white head proud and high, into the ring where cheers greeted him. In the race itself, the stands resounded to cheering as he put in extravagant leaps at the fences up the straight. He won unchallenged but nobody cared that it had been a schooling round. Nobody considered it an anti-climax.

The clan regathered at Kempton Park, three weeks later, for another race unashamedly designed to attract the money-spinning grey. They called it the Boxing Day Trial Chase, a perfectly reasonable idea as a prelude to the King George, run over the same course and distance. Not being a handicap, it drew the best horses and not many of them. Only three were left in at the overnight stage, Panto Prince and Sun Rising providing the opposition to Desert Orchid who had won the same race, in the same-sized field, a year earlier.

There was a hitch. The autumn had been unusually dry and the Kempton ground, which often rides fast, was officially firm. Elsworth left it late to make up his mind but, after walking the course at midday, he declared his star inmate a non-runner. Although not entirely unexpected, the announcement came as a massive disappointment to another big crowd. Elsworth, however, won the sympathy of everyone when he said: 'I felt it was too much of a risk. If I had run him and something had happened, I would never have forgiven myself.'

Elsworth's late decision granted no favours to his jockey. Sherwood had arranged to wait at a junction of the M4 for the verdict; if Desert Orchid was taken out, he would rush to Worcester to ride the promising novice chaser, Vicar's Landing, for his brother Oliver. When the call eventually came through on his car phone, time was exceedingly short and Sherwood, foot flat to the boards, fell foul of the Thames Valley constabulary. By the time he had

At the end of the season Desert Orchid won the Piper Champagne Award not only for Best Horse of the Year, but also for the Greatest Contribution to National Hunt Racing – both awards thoroughly justified. He received his award – an ice-bucket full of polo mints – at the Cheltenham April meeting, and there to share it with him were his 'lass', Janice Coyle, and Rodney Boult. Boult rarely goes racing: on the three occasions he has done so when Desert Orchid has been running, the horse has been inexplicably beaten, and Boult reckons that his presence on the racecourse puts a jinx on the grey. He tried going in disguise once, but the result was the same

concluded the painful interview he knew he had missed his ride.
Needless to add, Vicar's Landing won without him.

Sherwood's frustrated reaction to a wasted day was illuminating. Instead of going home to kick the cat, sulk in front of the
television or glare unhappily at all the food and drink he could not
possibly consume, he organized a band of friends for a night in
London . . . go-karting. Although there might easily have been
grounds for a stewards' enquiry into the running of several of the
races, Sherwood won the competition and conquered his sense of
aggravation.

By the following morning, he was looking ahead to the rest of
Desert Orchid's season and making public some firm views. 'I am
convinced he is now much better suited to 3 miles than 2,' he said.
'I also see no reason why he should not run in the Gold Cup, and
win it.'

Elsworth and Richard Burridge valued Sherwood's advice very
highly, though perhaps you might not have known it from what
happened next. Deprived of his run at Kempton, the horse was
returned to 2 miles for his next race – and in a handicap at that.
Meanwhile, both owner and trainer headed off the persistent enquiries about Cheltenham plans, determinedly non-committal
and, at least in Burridge's case, genuinely unsure that the Gold
Cup was a good idea.

Any fears that Desert Orchid, approaching his 11th birthday,
might no longer be able to give so much weight to some of the
best 2-mile handicappers in the country were proved groundless
at Sandown Park on 3 December. Carrying 12 stone, he made the
running as usual and, despite one mistake at the ninth, quickened
right away to score by twelve lengths from Jim Thorpe, who
received 20 pounds, and Panto Prince, receiving 18.

By comparison, he had almost to struggle to win his second
King George on Boxing Day – though all things are relative. It
was in this race, two years earlier, that Sherwood had ridden
Desert Orchid for the first time because Elsworth's stable jockey
Colin Brown, faced with an agonizing choice between two class
horses, wrongly opted for Combs Ditch. A year later, with
Brown back on board, Desert Orchid went off at even money
for the race but could finish only second to the French invader,
Nupsala. Many observers were inclined to blame Brown, arguing
that he should not have taken on Beau Ranger and Cybrandian in
a frantic battle for the lead over the first half of the race. It was sad
for Brown to come in for such criticism as his riding of the great
horse had usually been exemplary; still, it did nothing to dampen
his loyalty to the cause and, although busy running a successful
Berkshire pub, Brown was on hand at every one of Desert Orchid's races this season. Like the rest of us, he thrilled to a spectacu-

lar display of jumping at Kempton which eventually accounted for Kildimo, right back to his best, by four lengths.

Three weeks on (and this is the time regularly allotted to Desert Orchid between races), the roadshow moved on to Ascot, already the scene of seven previous wins. It is true that Elsworth has kept the horse to certain favoured courses: he had also, by this stage, scored eight wins at Sandown, five at Kempton and four at Wincanton. It had long been said that if the Gold Cup was run around Sandown or Ascot, he would win it every year. This next race on the agenda, however, was another case of Elsworth mixing the treatment, for it was back to 2 miles, this time attempting to give 22 pounds to Chris Popham's greatly improved Panto Prince.

It was a thriller, thought by some to be the race of the season and by some melodramatics to be the race of any other season, too. Panto Prince, ridden with style and spirit by Brendan Powell, was at his peak and, at several stages of the race, looked sure to win. Desert Orchid was unable to dictate as he likes to. Indeed,

In January Desert Orchid won the Victor Chandler Chase at Ascot after a fierce battle with Panto Prince. Sherwood for once did not enjoy the race, and neither did Desert Orchid, who was reverting to 2 miles. Brendan Powell on Panto Prince hassled them all the way round, and in the end there was only a neck in it. After the race Sherwood was relieved, and Janice Coyle and Jimmy Burridge, the horse's breeder (left), delighted

Panto Prince led from the fifth fence to the last and, although headed briefly by Desert Orchid, took it up again on the run-in. They raced for the line locked together, the Saturday crowd beside itself with excitement; they flashed past the post apparently in unison but Peter O'Sullevan, who is seldom wrong, called Desert Orchid first in his stirring commentary for BBC TV. The judge called for a photograph and the winning distance was a head.

The emotion of that day was equalled on 4 February when he registered his ninth Sandown win. Again, the fast ground ensured a small field, only four, but the Racecall Gainsborough Chase was another handicap and Desert Orchid, though back over 3 miles, was obliged to take on three potential Gold Cup rivals, Charter Party, Kildimo and Pegwell Bay, on much less favourable terms than he would at Cheltenham.

Kildimo was expected to provide the main danger but, having fallen at the previous Sandown meeting, he was not at his best. Charter Party, winner of the 1988 Gold Cup, was still more out of sorts and the finish concerned Desert Orchid and Pegwell Bay, the star of the early-season 2½-mile handicaps but now tackling 3 miles for the first time. In some ways it was a replica of the Ascot race. Pegwell Bay, jumping, if anything, still more flamboyantly than his opponent, took up the running at the twelfth fence and was not headed until the last. Then, just as the crowd expected Desert Orchid's proven staying ability to decide the issue, Pegwell Bay rallied heroically and had the effrontery to pass the grey again. The thing about Desert Orchid, however, is that the notion of accepting defeat gracefully has no meaning for him. He quickened again, insulted to find himself chasing this upstart, and this time had three-quarters of a length to spare at the line.

The crowd gave voice to its feelings; someone called for three cheers in the unsaddling enclosure and the response was deafening. But now, intriguingly, the appeal of this unique horse had spread inwards from the public to the hard-nosed professionals. Jockeys who had not been riding in the race, marched out of the comfortable Sandown weighing-room to stand on the balcony applauding Desert Orchid. They were unanimous in the view that racing at large was benefiting enormously from the emotion generated by this one horse.

If there was a sadness it was that Pegwell Bay, having run out-standingly well, was almost ignored in defeat. As his trainer Tim Forster ruefully remarked: 'On any other course, against any other horse, we would have won. But Desert Orchid is one of those amazing animals who can sprint up the Sandown hill at the end of 3 miles.'

And so to Cheltenham. The die was cast and the target would be the Gold Cup. Elsworth, of course, wanted to run Barnbrook

The tension shows on Simon Sherwood's face as Desert Orchid is led out for the parade prior to the Gold Cup. The ground was totally unsuitable for the grey, and although David Elsworth was convinced he could handle it, Sherwood had promised Richard Burridge that he would pull Desert Orchid up if the horse felt unhappy

Again in the 2-mile Queen Mother Chase (he won it) and did not want his stars clashing, but there was also a feeling that this was so much Desert Orchid's season that ducking the Gold Cup would be cheating everyone, close connections included.

If Richard Burridge retained any slight reservations he hid them well . . . at least until the day of the race. Then, it was as if the elements had conspired to produce a scenario sure to deny us the climax everyone wanted to see. There had been snow overnight and now rain was hammering down on the already heavy ground. Burridge, who had walked the course in the early morning, did not like what he had seen and as the day wore on his features increasingly took on the furrows of a severely worried man.

Rumours spread around the course, as they always do in times

As the field is about to start the second circuit Desert Orchid has established a short lead from Ten Plus, followed by Yahoo (left) and Charter Party

of adversity. It was said that Desert Orchid would not run, which was unarguably in Burridge's mind. It was also said that racing was about to be abandoned, which would have suited the anxious owner extremely well. Burridge was tracked by a posse of cameramen and journalists as he sought out David Elsworth. The trainer, when he arrived, proved to be calmness itself and, with a stewards' inspection already successfully concluded, the spectre of disappointment was lifted. Elsworth, Burridge and Sherwood consulted: trainer said reassuringly to owner, 'If he isn't liking it, Simon will pull him up after two fences. Don't worry.' Burridge smiled, and worried like hell.

Only when it was over did a smile crack his features and then, you suspected, it had been preceded by tears. If he had wept with the joy of the moment, Burridge was far from alone. Desert Orchid had conquered the elements, the ground, the left-handed track and, most courageously, the tigerish attentions of a horse called Yahoo.

Prior to the race Richard Burridge was extremely concerned for the welfare of Desert Orchid in the heavy ground. His relief and admiration are apparent in the unsaddling enclosure, as the horse – mud-spattered and ears pricked – is, as usual, acutely aware of everything going on around him

John Edwards had thought highly of this horse since bringing him south from the stables of Jack Hanson. He won three times in the 1987–88 season and his target this term was always the Gold Cup, though he seldom did himself justice in preliminary races through absence of the soft ground he needs. At Cheltenham, it was as soft as raceable ground can be and a few canny punters plunged on Yahoo as the morning rains persisted. They were thwarted only after a spectacular scrap.

Nobody will ever convince Kevin Mooney that Ten Plus might not have held on to the lead he had poached going to the third last. Nobody, probably, will persuade Richard Rowe that his classy outsider Ballyhane would not have continued the menacing progress he had made coming down the hill to that notorious fence. But Ten Plus fell, fatally, and Ballyhane was unluckily brought down.

This left Desert Orchid in front as the field, or what remained of it, completed the descent and turned for home. It was short-lived. Yahoo, travelling sweetly through the mire, quickly took up the running and jumped the last still holding a half-length lead. Not for the first time, however, Desert Orchid showed that he can battle from behind just as capably as blaze a trail. The crowd, a record for Cheltenham's feature day, exploded in noise as the grey came again up the hill and won, going away, by one-and-a-half lengths. What followed was familiar only to those who had been present on that incredible day when Dawn Run won the Gold Cup and half of Ireland, it seemed, followed him into the winner's enclosure. The English being a shade more reserved, there may not quite have been the volume of people crushing through the barriers, but the tearful emotion was at least as intense.

Burridge himself was overcome. He said he could not see the last part of the race because his binoculars had steamed up. 'I listened to the noise of the crowd and they told me the result,' he said. 'It was simply amazing. Desert Orchid is a great horse, with an incredible gift.'

Elsworth recovered enough to say: 'I was always confident we had made the right decision to run. Next year's Gold Cup might be abandoned and the year after, Dessie could have a bad leg.' It was a phlegmatic trainer's response to a charged situation, but he was right, so very right.

There might possibly have been a more popular and more courageous winner of the Gold Cup but, as dank afternoon turned to night, nobody could remember one. Perhaps the last word should belong to Simon Sherwood, who said: 'Yahoo was going so well at the second last that any other horse would have thrown in the towel. Dessie is the best and bravest horse I've ever ridden.'

It was at Aintree, a year earlier, that Desert Orchid finally won on a left-handed course for the first time and fuelled speculation that he just might be a Gold Cup horse after all. This year, with the main business at Cheltenham done and his reputation as the finest steeplechaser in Britain established beyond dispute, Aintree was a lone disappointment. Although his jumping here looks spectacular enough, the grim expression on Simon Sherwood's face tells much about the feel he was getting from a tired horse. When he fell, the gasp could have been heard across Merseyside. It was Sherwood's only defeat on Desert Orchid, a sad way for a great partnership to end

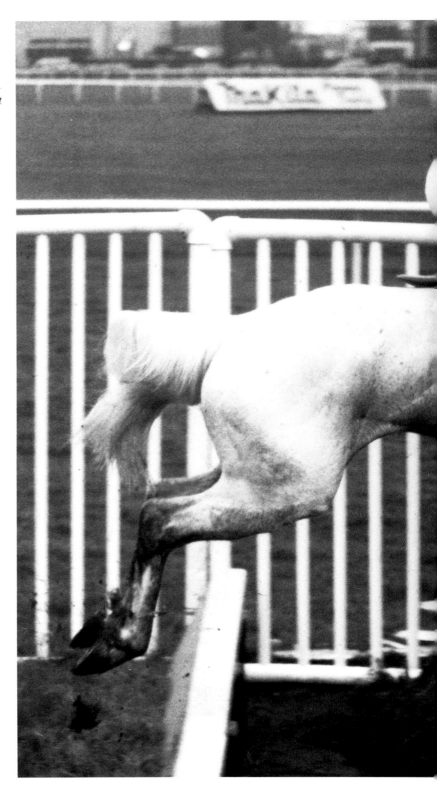

Concern shows on the faces of Richard Burridge and Janice Coyle as they retrieve their fallen idol. It was the one moment of grief in Desert Orchid's season

Riding to a fall. Still in front, but showing little of his usual spark, Desert Orchid is destined to come to grief at the next fence on Aintree's Mildmay course

At home in Whitsbury and plainly at peace with the world – the racehorse of the year

CHAPTER FIVE

The Cheltenham Festival

A sight to stir the emotions of any racing man – the parade ring at Cheltenham on a sparkling spring day, the terraces packed with keen, expectant faces and the horsewalk populated only by animals who have earned their place in the world's most elite gathering of National Hunt horses. There are major meetings every week of the jumping season . . . but there is only one Festival

Nobody, and I include the horse's connections, had seriously regarded Beech Road as a Champion Hurdle contender until he beat Guy Harwood's highly respected Vagador in a minor race at Fontwell Park. Even then, most good judges dismissed the form as irrelevant and concentrated on the illustrious horses at the head of the betting market – Sheikh Mohammed's unbeaten Kribensis, reigning champion Celtic Shot and Mercy Rimell's classy

contender Celtic Chief. Beech Road, it was widely agreed, could not win – after all, he was a failed novice chaser who, on his previous appearance at Cheltenham, had winded himself so badly on falling at the last fence that the screens were erected around him. He rose in time to cheat death and, on the first day of the 1989 Festival, he came on the scene like a brass-necked gatecrasher at a gala party, winning with an ease which struck silence across the

sardine-packed stands. Kribensis, labouring in the rain-softened ground, was a spent force between the last two flights and, for a moment, it seemed that triumph would go to Mole Board, recently transferred to West Country trainer Jim Old and heavily backed before the off. At the last, however, it was all over. Beech Road, the imposter, the horse who could not win, jumped past Mole Board without even engaging top gear and strode away up the hill

*Beech Road was returned at 50/1
but, if trainer Toby Balding had
never given the impression he
expected to be in the winner's
enclosure, his young jockey Richard
Guest had always believed in the
possibility. Or so he said. Guest, the
latest member of a racing dynasty and
described by Balding as 'an embryo
star', rode the horse with utmost
confidence, a quality he also
displayed later in the hubbub which
greeted his triumphant return*

Peter Scudamore considered Sabin du Loir his banker of the Festival. Martin Pipe's exciting novice was established as firm favourite for the Arkle Chase on the opening day and there were many who would not hear of defeat. Beaten he was, however, by the horse upsides him here as the field turns away from the stands. Waterloo Boy (left) started the season in the modest company of a Worcester handicap but, brought along slowly by trainer David Nicholson, he did very little wrong and arrived at the Festival as a lively outsider. To the great chagrin of Scudamore, he outstayed both Sabin du Loir and the northern challenger Southern Minstrel up the hill

Day one had not gone well for Scudamore. He could have ridden the Pipe-trained winner of the first event, the Supreme Novices Hurdle, but chose to ride the Irish fancy Elementary, who fell. He was beaten on several more fancied rides before winning the Grand Annual Chase with an inspired performance on Pukka Major. On day two, the sun shone – but not for the champion. For the second day in succession he chose wrongly and missed a Pipe winner. Sayfars Lad, partnered by the able Mark Perrett (pictured), won the Sun Alliance Novices Hurdle. Scudamore finished last on the stable's other runner, Pertemps Network

The smart-soled gent on his knees is not actually giving praise to the equine feats of past Gold Cup hero Golden Miller. At least, we don't think so. Along with his three stocky colleagues, he is examining means of fixing the new statue in position for the grand unveiling

A sea of raised binoculars, hopeful expressions and, in certain cases, empty pockets . . .

*A meeting of the Irish racing minds
. . . Richard Dunwoody's father
(left) discusses the state of the game
with one of the most famous Irishmen
who ever lived, Pat Taaffe. In every
bar and every available cranny of this
great course, such reunions take
place. Cheltenham, as somebody once
said, is a week when you see real
friends you never meet at any other
time of year*

*One of the week's most thrilling
finishes decided the Sun Alliance
Chase for staying novices. Nick the
Brief, owned by Midlands building
magnate John Upson, led most of the
3-mile trip but was headed on
landing over the last by Josh
Gifford's 16/1 shot Envopak
Token (near side). They duelled all
the way up the hill, Envopak
Token holding on by a length with
Brown Windsor, who went on to
win the Whitbread Gold Cup, close
up third*

There had been a widespread tendency to forget what a shrewd trainer, especially of handicappers, Martin Tate can be. Times had been quiet for the Kidderminster farmer but on the sunlit middle day of the Festival, he pulled off the gamble of the week with Roger's Princess, a staying mare. This horse's name had been on informed lips for some weeks before Cheltenham; there were those who considered she had been 'thrown in' the handicap for the Coral Golden Hurdle Final, run over a demanding 3 miles 1 furlong. Huge ante-post wagers were struck, bringing her price down from the philanthropic 25/1 to the merely generous 12/1. Such furious gambles, such reputed 'good things', come to grief more often than not. This one, however, gave her followers very few anxious moments and left the rest of a competitive field for dead on the run-in to score by twelve lengths. For Martin and Edna Tate, two of the genuine sorts who characterize National Hunt racing, it was a welcome and widely popular return to big-race glory. For the bookmaker owner of Roger's Princess, it was an extremely profitable pay-day

Richard Rowe's season did not proceed to plan. Stable jockey to Josh Gifford, whose yard in picturesque Findon houses one of the most powerful jumping strings in Britain, Rowe looked forward to more big winners than he had ever ridden in his life and, quite conceivably, to helping Gifford achieve an elusive ambition by becoming champion trainer. Martin Pipe clinically saw off the latter notion but the first was cheated by a conspiracy of events. All was going well until, in December, Rowe broke his ankle in a fall at Huntingdon from the novice chaser Staghound. In his absence, Gifford's best horses spectacularly chorused their well-being and deputy jockey Peter Hobbs rode a four-timer at Cheltenham's December meeting.

He also won the valuable SGB Chase at Ascot on Ballyhane, a horse Gifford believed (against popular judgement but, as it transpired, correctly) to be a genuine Gold Cup prospect. Rowe fought back to active service, but his return coincided with a downturn in the yard's fortunes. Then, to his own justifiable dismay, he was injured once again. His second comeback, hastened by natural incentives, brought him to the Festival physically fit but with a question-mark over his confidence, which defeats on the fancied Clay Hill and Green Willow, plus a fall from Vodkatini in the Queen Mother Champion Chase, did nothing to allay. Gifford himself, though traditionally loyal to his jockeys, went public on the concern. Hobbs

was given the ride on Envopak Token in the Sun Alliance Chase, and won. Rowe went out to partner Paddyboro in Wednesday's final race, the Mildmay of Flete Handicap Chase, knowing that he stood to lose the Gold Cup mount on Ballyhane unless his luck turned. It did. In the familiar cherry-red colours, Rowe was visibly oozing confidence and Paddyboro came home one of the most impressive winners of the week. Gifford, relieved beyond words, instantly confirmed that he would be Ballyhane's partner. Rowe retired to sip a meditative glass of champagne and ponder on just what a turbulent job his can be

Gold Cup day, and the weather was unspeakable . . . up in the hills around Cheltenham, where dozens of hotels provide the Festival beds for thousands of racegoers, breakfast-time was dominated by doubts and depression as snow fell thickly and persistently outside the misted windows. Some, weary from two days of battling with claustrophobia and dubious of the pleasures awaiting them now, spoke of giving up and going home – only to be talked out of such folly by more indomitable friends. Others doubted whether the day's racing would even take place. They had a fair point. Although the course itself escaped all but a few flurries of snow, rain had fallen relentlessly and the stewards called a precautionary inspection at noon. By then, of course, many of the 50,000 spectators had already arrived, the sensible abandoning all pretence at finery and donning Wellingtons to wade through car parks which had become a sea of mud

. . . And so the racing went ahead, though not in any great comfort. The members' lawn, in front of the stands, is a favoured vantage point for many racegoers. On Gold Cup day, any who ventured there knew at once they were writing off another pair of shoes

Out on the course, one particular area at the foot of the hill was causing real concern. Philip Arkwright, the capable clerk of the course, resorted to last-ditch measures and called in the local fire brigade to pump the surface water away

In ground now officially heavy, the juveniles' championship race, the Daily Express Triumph Hurdle, was always likely to throw up a sensation. Traditionally run at a demanding pace and with the accent on stamina, it was now a merciless examination of a horse's bravery. Some of the class horses were far from disgraced: Sheikh Mohammed's Highland Bud was second, Jenny Pitman's hope Don Valentino third and Royal Derbi, running his thirteenth race in a season which had begun on the rock-hard ground of Plumpton in August, fourth. The winner (pictured at the final flight) was initially stunning – Ikdam, trained in the West Country by Richard Holder, had won only once over hurdles and, in his preceding race, had been beaten twelve lengths into fourth on similarly heavy ground at Haydock. The key to his success, however, is that his win was gained over 2½ miles in the Uttoxeter mud. Ikdam is a thorough stayer and when other, faster horses had simply exhausted their reserves, he was still running on dourly for the biggest four-year-old prize of the season. The form was reversed once more six weeks later when, at Ireland's annual Punchestown Festival, Ikdam could finish only fourth behind Royal Derbi and Highland Bud. His connections knew, however, that he had won the race which mattered and, as jockey Nigel Coleman commented: 'He'll probably need 3 miles next season'

If the 1989 Gold Cup day will never be forgotten due to Desert Orchid, it will also be rightly remembered for Three Counties. Nothing could have been more appropriate than the triumph of the game, mud-loving twelve-year-old in the Christies Foxhunters Chase – the amateurs' Gold Cup. He was trained by Mrs Mercy Rimell, on her final operative day at the Festival, and ridden by Mercy's 25-year-old granddaughter Katie. If the winner's enclosure scenes were exuberant, emotional and even tinged with tears, there was good reason, for this was more than just another family success. Mrs Rimell retired at the end of the 1988-89 season – not by choice, but because her landlords declined to renew the lease on her Worcestershire yard. Quite how she would get along without the sport which had filled her life ever more since the sad death of her legendary husband Fred, was something Mercy did not wish to contemplate. A sensitive lady beneath the veneer which has her wrongly categorized as 'formidable' in so many minds, she dreaded the end of what was almost half a century of racing involvement. Katie's win on Three Counties at least ensured her a very special memory to take with her into retirement

After two days of grim weather, during which the ground on the Grand National course had changed from soft to bog-like, the great day dawned blissfully sunny. A post-war record crowd of more than 70,000, emphasising yet again the increased popularity of jump racing and the magnetic pulling power of its most famous event, poured through the Aintree gates and took their places in the once-a-year stands. For many, this is a rare relationship with racing but for others it is an annual pilgrimage, which involves rather more than watching the action. Grand National week is a social must in the diaries of many racing folk; they fill a series of hotels in the drowsy coastal town of Southport, all of which are urgently spruced up for the invasion, and they eat and drink in huge, convivial parties before catching a few hours sleep and emerging, remarkably bright-eyed, for the morning drive to Aintree and the resumption of the ritual. For many, this is the best week of the year, with the National itself as its centrepiece

CHAPTER SIX

The Grand National

A FAVOURITE GAME AMONG RACING SCRIBES, in the days leading
up to each year's Grand National, is to nominate the
'story'. For the National, more than any other horse-race and
perhaps any other sporting event in the calendar, always pro-
vides a story, be it romantic, nostalgic, dramatic or ironical.
Show me the National which had the assembled press scratching
their heads for an angle, and I will show you an imposter.

The 1989 race had all manner of possibilities. It was, sadly, the
first National since the untimely death of John Hughes, whose
boundless energy and innovative mind had been the driving force
behind the revitalized Aintree. Would it not be appropriate if the
race was won by Dixton House, owned in partnership by one of
John's greatest friends; or even by Jenny Pitman's Gainsay, whose
stable lad just happens to be called John Hughes?

Alternatively, everyone – no matter the direction of their betting money – would applaud victory for Gala's Image, the last
National runner for the Rimell family after Mercy, widow of
four-times winning trainer Fred, had been unceremoniously
forced into retirement by the landlords of her Worcestershire
yard.

There were headline possibilities about Newnham, winner of
the Aintree Foxhunters a year ago and again ridden by the young
amateur, Simon Andrews, and about Numerate, sold just days
before the race in order to give a first National ride to Tarnya
Davis. There was more, emotionally more, to Tarnya's story
than simply being the latest lady rider to tackle the National. Eight
months earlier her boyfriend, the talented young jockey Paul

The 1988 race had been won by
David Elsworth's Rhyme 'n'
Reason, ridden with style and
strength by the Lambourn-based
Irishman, Brendan Powell. No-one
who saw it, at the time or on the
oft-repeated slow-motion replay,
will forget the way in which Powell
hoisted his horse off the floor after
an apparently terminal mistake at
the formidable Becher's Brook. This
time, Powell was aboard Stearsby,
a horse he had himself helped to
acquire for the rising Somerset
trainer, Gerald Ham. Stearsby was
furiously supported in the betting
market in the days leading up to the
race and, with Powell taking him
along the far outside, he was soon
in front. He jumped Becher's
immaculately, as the picture shows,
but two fences later he came
shudderingly to grief

Croucher, had been killed in a horrific car crash. Tarnya was only slowly coming to terms with her loss, but she saw the National ride as a tribute to Paul and even wore a sweater belonging to him under her silks.

The 150th National winner turned out to be none of these. On a warm, sunlit and appropriately perfect April day, utterly at odds with the grim weather of the preceding 48 hours, the winner of the marathon was a twelve-year-old veteran of three previous Nationals. Little Polveir had not previously been so much as placed in the race but, 12 months earlier, he had been travelling ominously well at the head of affairs when he parted company with jockey Tom Morgan five from home.

It is here that the 'story' of 1989 begins to emerge, for Morgan is the retained jockey of John Edwards, who had trained Little Polveir all his racing life, won a Scottish Grand National with him and prepared him for those three abortive Aintree tilts. Just six weeks before the 1989 race, however, Little Polveir left Edwards' base in Ross-on-Wye to join the thriving, dual-purpose yard of Toby Balding in the Hampshire village of Fyfield. And, while Edwards suffered the disappointment of seeing his two runners, Dixton House and Bob Tisdall, come to grief early in the race, it was nothing to his mortification at the sight of Little Polveir storming to triumph along that daunting, 494-yard run-in.

Edwards, characteristic of National Hunt sportsmen, took his punishment well and was among the first to congratulate the horse's new connections. His private thoughts may have been unprintable; so too, those of jockey Morgan, who had undergone a week of spartan dieting and vigorous exercise in order to shed 11 pounds and ride Dixton House. The 7/1 favourite got no further than Becher's, first time around.

Becher's was, unfortunately, responsible for further controversy in the wake of two fatal falls. The Irish horse, Seeandem, and Brown Trix (also, ironically, in the charge of winning trainer Balding) were both put down after falling backwards into the ditch following bad mistakes. The RSPCA pledged to press for the slope on the landing side of the fence to be levelled out, while Balding proposed, at his champagne party the day after the race, that the brook itself should be filled in. Such incidents cannot lightly be ignored; most would agree they are an unacceptably high price to pay for the retention of tradition and that the National would not suffer any great identity crisis through the simple rearrangement of one, albeit famous, landmark. The Jockey Club agreed and work on the changes is underway.

If these were the sad tales of National day, there were as ever many happy ones. Balding himself was walking on air, for not only had he won the great race, he had added to that the £20,000-

Some were not so lucky at Becher's. Brown Trix, once trained by Fred Winter, was bought by the fanatical amateur, David Pitcher, with the Grand National in mind. Although past the age of 50, and although he had not even begun riding until 48, Pitcher lined up in the race. The instructions of his trainer, Toby Balding, were simply to keep out of the way. He took the far outside but Becher's brought him down. Pitcher himself was kicked in the face and his horse, desperately winded, slid back into the ditch and could not be revived. The incident led to concerted calls for a rethink of the traditional fence, a levelling-off of the landing side and even the filling-in of the ditch and brook

Seeandem, an Irish challenger, did not survive the Becher's Brook drop, either, as Colin Turner's spectacular picture shows

plus prize for the Sandeman Aintree Hurdle through his insultingly under-rated champion Beech Road, and rounded off an astonishingly successful day with the final hurdle, won by a certain star of the future in Morley Street.

Jimmy Frost rode Morley Street, 90 minutes after returning in glory on Little Polveir, and it is another of the day's charming ironies that he was later to admit: 'Morley Street is so clearly the classiest horse I have ever ridden that I was actually scared of getting a fall in the National and being unable to ride him!'

Frost need not have worried. Little Polveir knows his way around Liverpool and made only one mistake, at the imposing ditch which is 19th on the programme. 'He was so clever he got in close and climbed over it,' explained Frost who, by this stage of the race, had banished all thoughts of self-preservation as the ultimate jumping prize loomed. 'I kept thinking "this isn't happening",' he said. 'I told myself to keep cool and concentrate, but the horse did the work for me.'

Little Polveir had taken up the running at the water jump, down below the stands at the end of the first circuit, and he never surrendered the initiative. Nor, in truth, did he look likely to be caught, despite the successive efforts of such highly fancied rivals as Smart Tar, Bonanza Boy, West Tip, Lastofthebrownies and, finally, Durham Edition.

A year earlier, Durham Edition had led over the last, the race

West Tip knows his way around the National course better than any horse alive, the veteran Red Rum naturally excepted. Four previous attempts had brought him a win, a place, a fall and a gallant completion. This time, the suspicion persisted that trainer Michael Oliver was asking him one question too many. Oliver, however, knew better and West Tip so plainly enjoyed himself that another bid in 1990 is now being considered. He looked the likely winner a mile from home but lost his place briefly before tigerishly coming again on the run-in to snatch second place, under the jockey who has ridden him in all five of his Nationals, Richard Dunwoody

apparently in the pocket of the northern 'rambo', Chris Grant. Only on that merciless run-in did Arthur Stephenson's horse give best to Rhyme 'n' Reason, relegating Grant to the runner's-up berth for the second time. Now, as they jumped the 30th and last fence in the 1989 version, Durham Edition was at Little Polveir's flank, surely ready to pick him off and justify the heavy betting support which had sent him away at 15/2 second favourite. But it was not to be. Durham Edition simply failed to see out the trip in the heavy ground and could finish only fifth.

At the elbow, half-way down the run-in, Little Polveir's only danger seemed to come from West Tip, who had lost his pitch between the last two fences but was now conjuring up a staggering burst of speed, narrowing the gap with every stride. It was here that Frost needed divine intervention and found it in the form of Smart Tar. His National hopes had ended with a fall at the 19th, but he completed the course riderless and his presence, loping along on the rails side, inspired Little Polveir to a final effort. He was not going to be beaten, even by a horse without a jockey.

Frost was naturally enough the subject of all manner of tributes, not least from Balding. Asked how their apparently improbable liaison had begun, he cracked: 'I needed a real horseman to ride a horse called Lucky Vane – long legs and no brain, just the ticket.' In more private moments, however, Balding told what he really thought of the bashful Jimmy, who for most of his thirteen years in racing had been confined to point-to-points or rides on the Devon circuit and had never even come close to riding in the National before.

'I had watched Jimmy riding down in the west and often thought what a lovely horseman he was,' recalled Balding. 'Lucky Vane started us off but he was then engaged to ride Kildimo, who may yet turn out to be a Gold Cup horse. Before this season began we talked about a retainer but I'm afraid Jimmy is equally as businesslike as me and we have done nothing about it. You may rest assured, though, that he will be retained for next year.'

There were plenty of people in the Balding camp who had considered Little Polveir a very good National prospect. Frost was among them, though it transpired his reasons were unorthodox. 'The winning jockey is presented with a car by Citroen,' explained Balding, 'and when he came to ride out Little Polveir three days before the race, Jimmy told me he was sure to win because he had just bought a new car.'

Another who had every confidence was Fiona Hambleton, the 'lad' who looks after Little Polveir. 'She had every right to be optimistic,' said Balding, 'because she has been so lucky for us. Every horse she has done has won a race, and it is no accident. She is very kind to them and they respond. This horse was a bit fed up

All the colour and spectacle of the National is captured by this view of the formidable Chair. Little Polveir and West Tip, very much the old hands, jump either side of the outsider, Mithras

with life when he arrived in the yard but Fiona has helped to sweeten him up.'

The best background story of the race, however, concerned the reasons and the methods by which Little Polveir found his way to Fyfield where, exactly 20 years earlier, Balding had celebrated his only previous National winner, Highland Wedding. It is perhaps best told in the words of Ted Harvey, the 54-year-old owner. Ted has farms in Hertfordshire and in Galloway; he rode in point-to-points until his constant battle against weight finally defeated his enthusiasm; and his only previous horse in training had been 'not very successful' in Newmarket.

'This all began when my son David, who is an army captain serving in Germany, spoke about finding a horse to ride in San-down's Grand Military Gold Cup. David is six feet two inches tall and weighs all of 13 stone out of season, so I reasoned that if he was willing to make sacrifices to do the weight, his father ought to support him. He was on leave for five weeks so we set off at the crack of dawn one February day to see various horses in different corners of the country, each of which had been recommended by Toby as being suitable for the job.

'We arrived at Ross-on-Wye before 8 a.m. Little Polveir was the first one we saw but we both liked him immediately. Although we drove about 2000 miles in the week, looked at two of Arthur Stephenson's in Bishop Auckland and several others besides, we

Toby Balding, urbane, experienced and articulate, has been here before – 20 years ago with Highland Wedding. Jimmy Frost, 30-year-old farmer's son from Dartmoor who turned professional almost as an afterthought, never expected to be here at all . . . such is the magic of the National

both came back to Little Polveir as our selection. He did the job, too, giving David a memorable ride to finish fourth in a good-class race. He was already entered for the National so, although he was not bought with the race in mind, it seemed foolish not to run him – especially as he had been going so well last year.'

This was the point that most judges appeared to miss in sifting through the innumerable options for their big-race tip. If the ideal virtues of a National horse are substantial experience and in-exhaustible stamina, few if any could match the claims of Little Polveir. Only West Tip had been round more than three times in the National, and he finished a gallant second. No accident, this, for in conditions such as prevailed this year, experience was every-thing.

As Little Polveir goes for home, Peter Scudamore tries to rally Bonanza Boy (pink colours) while Neale Doughty makes his challenge in the red and black colours of Mercy Rimell's Gala's Image

What of the other potential fairy-tales? Well, Mercy Rimell's Gala's Image ran with great credit and completed in seventh place, his chance finally extinguished by the going. Tarnya Davis and Numerate pulled up at the 21st, promising to be back next year. John Hughes, the lad, took Gainsay home with similar hopes after a fall at the 19th. As for the owners of Dixton House, considered a handicap certainty by the formbook buffs after his facile, unpenalized win at the Cheltenham Festival, they must have driven thoughtfully home contemplating the reality that, in the Grand National, a 'good thing' exists only in the imagination.

Little Polveir jumps the last with Durham Edition (Chris Grant) in close attendance. For Grant, it was to be another case of so near, yet so far. Second twice, on Young Driver in 1986 and on Durham Edition in 1988, he appeared to have the race at his mercy when he came to challenge the long-time leader between the last two fences. As he had feared all week, however, the state of the ground had got to the bottom of his horse's stamina and he faded on that punishing run-in

The loose horse with the white face, ears pricked as if he thinks he has won the race, is Smart Tar. He had been travelling easily when parting company with jockey Carl Llewellyn but was enjoying himself so much that he carried on around the course. Jimmy Frost was grateful. Little Polveir had been alone in front for a very long time and the run-in was taking its toll when the sight and sound of Smart Tar ranging alongside galvanized him to one last burst, seeing off all the horses with riders, as well as the riderless one

*Simon Sherwood teamed up with
the enduring northern maestro,
Arthur Stephenson, to win the
Whitbread Trophy Chase,
traditionally the first race of the
meeting over National fences.
Villierstown went off a well-backed
favourite and Sherwood gave him
a textbook ride to win easily from a
disappointing field*

*The Foxhunters race is Friday's
spectacular over the National
course. The horses are seasoned
hunters, used to jumping a whole
variety of obstacles, but the jockeys
are amateurs and, frequently,
old-fashioned in their style. Here
are two views of this season's winner,
Call Collect, and his rider*

In mid-season, Golden Freeze, a novice over fences, was being trumpeted as a potential Gold Cup winner. It was premature talk but, Jenny Pitman being a formidable trainer of big-race winners, it may transpire to be prophetic, judging by this bold-jumping horse's impressive win on the Friday programme

When Jimmy Fitzgerald fancies one, his followers are seldom disappointed and Mark Dwyer (right), stylish as ever, ensured that the gamble on Hill Street did not go astray

*Monica Dickinson's last big
winner, Travel Over, clears the
last with ears pricked*

TOP JUMPS HORSES 1988–89

IN WIN PRIZEMONEY ORDER

HORSE/BREEDER	WIN PRIZEMONEY	PLACE PRIZEMONEY	TOTAL PRIZEMONEY	WINS-RUNS
DESERT ORCHID *J.D. Burridge*	£159,448	–	£159,448	6–7
BEECH ROAD *J. Tilling*	£75,995	£257	£76,252	3–8
BARNBROOK AGAIN *Ennistown Stud*	£73,151	–	£73,151	4–4
LITTLE POLVEIR *F.G. Harris*	£70,046	£1,935	£71,981	2–9
GREY SALUTE (CAN) *E.P. Taylor*	£51,914	£1,508	£53,422	3–7
ROLL-A-JOINT *R. Delaney*	£51,125	£1,665	£52,790	7–10
BROWN WINDSOR *W. Shand-Kydd*	£50,135	£8,218	£58,353	3–6
BONANZA BOY *Mrs K.M. Jeffery*	£48,788	£5,288	£54,076	3–7
PEGWELL BAY *G. Burr*	£46,528	£7,260	£53,788	3–5
WATERLOO BOY *M. and T. O'Brien and D. Magnier*	£46,513	£3,090	£49,603	6–7

TOP JUMPS JOCKEYS 1988–89

WINS-RIDES		JOCKEY AND LOWEST RIDING WEIGHT SINCE JAN 1 1988	TRAINER GIVING MOST WINNERS	WINS-RIDES	
221–663	33%	P. SCUDAMORE 10–0	M.C. Pipe	158–359	44%
92–457	20%	M. DWYER 10–0	J.G. FitzGerald	39–155	25%
91–671	14%	R. DUNWOODY 10–0	D. Nicholson	29–235	12%
86–425	20%	G. McCOURT 10–3	N. Tinkler	43–125	34%
68–317	21%	S. SHERWOOD 10–2	O. Sherwood	34–147	23%
64–583	11%	B. POWELL 10–0	G.A. Ham	17–59	29%
51–247	21%	T. MORGAN 10–1	J.A.C. Edwards	49–204	24%
50–462	11%	H. DAVIES 10–3	Capt. T.A. Forster	14–91	15%
49–340	14%	P. NIVEN 10–0	Mrs G.R. Reveley	18–122	15%
47–349	13%	PETER HOBBS 10–0	J.T. Gifford	27–115	23%
45–291	15%	S. SMITH ECCLES 10–3	J.S. King	7–32	22%
41–283	14%	J. FROST 10–1	G.B. Balding	25–152	16%
40–172	23%	M. PITMAN 10–5	Mrs J. Pitman	39–160	24%
39–192	20%	C. GRANT 10–0	W.A. Stephenson	33–130	25%
36–227	16%	L. WYER 10–0	M.H. Easterby	20–74	27%
34–215	16%	G. BRADLEY 10–4	D. Murray-Smith	15–65	23%
33–161	20%	N. DOUGHTY 10–4	G. Richards	20–62	32%
33–181	18%	M. HAMMOND 10–1	G.M. Moore	19–105	18%
32–256	13%	R. GOLDSTEIN 10–0	R. Curtis	10–70	14%
31–190	16%	DALE McKEOWN 10–0	R. Akehurst	27–110	25%

TOP JUMPS TRAINERS 1988–89

WINS-RUNS		TRAINER	WIN PRIZEMONEY	WIN & PLACE PRIZEMONEY	2ND	3RD	£1 STAKE PROFIT/LOSS
208–566	37%	M.C. PIPE	£589,460	£683,654	78	44	+72.63
54–255	21%	D.R.C. ELSWORTH	£359,990	£432,452	39	30	−12.01
59–371	16%	G.B. BALDING	£312,924	£406,974	51	32	−2.23
64–384	17%	J.T. GIFFORD	£293,984	£397,006	54	39	−65.33
78–402	19%	J.A.C. EDWARDS	£245,741	£383,360	64	45	+122.57
90–549	16%	W.A. STEPHENSON	£236,074	£353,485	76	76	−161.36
59–258	23%	J.G. FITZGERALD	£187,118	£228,876	45	24	−5.35
43–244	18%	N.J. HENDERSON	£170,460	£229,136	43	23	+1.22
62–279	22%	MRS J. PITMAN	£153,163	£211,410	36	33	+23.10
53–251	21%	O. SHERWOOD	£148,351	£204,124	43	31	+29.49
39–347	11%	D. NICHOLSON	£122,989	£231,196	58	45	−163.06
69–351	20%	G. RICHARDS	£119,190	£193,597	68	39	−57,68
34–231	15%	CAPT. T.A. FORSTER ..	£115,219	£153,873	23	30	−3.78
41–193	21%	C.P.E. BROOKS	£110,963	£169,247	35	26	−51.29
45–182	25%	M.H. EASTERBY	£109,273	£148,781	30	21	−27.39
29–287	10%	J.R. JENKINS	£100,397	£138,604	39	41	−115.33
43–201	21%	R. AKEHURST	£95,752	£128,129	26	18	+23.95
35–117	30%	D. MURRAY-SMITH	£86,022	£108,999	19	11	+52.44
20–135	15%	C.L. POPHAM	£84,791	£116,368	22	10	+9.78
29–185	16%	R. LEE	£79,060	£124,028	30	16	+42.32

TOP JUMPS OWNERS 1988–89

OWNER	HORSE WITH MOST WIN & PLACE PRIZEMONEY	1ST	2ND	3RD	4TH	WIN PRIZE
1 MR R. BURRIDGE .... (Desert Orchid)		8	3	2	1	£163.094
2 MR P. PILLER .... (Nautical Joke)		30	24	23	25	£83,591
3 MR TONY GEAKE .... (Beech Road)		3	–	–	1	£75,995
4 MR MEL DAVIES .... (Barnbrook Again)		4	–	–	–	£73,151
5 MR EDWARD HARVEY .... (Little Polveir)		1	–	–	1	£66,840
6 MR S. DUNSTER .... (Bonanza Boy)		7	1	–	1	£58,431
7 MR TONY HAYWARD .... (Grey Salute (CAN))		3	1	–	–	£51,914
8 MR RHYS THOMAS WILLIAMS .... (Roll-A-Joint)		7	1	1	–	£51,125
9 MR ROBERT WALEY-COHEN .... (Rustle)		8	3	4	1	£50,865
10 SHEIKH MOHAMMED .... (Kribensis)		6	2	–	–	£50,489

Peter Scudamore's Record 200 Winners

	DATE	COURSE	WINNER	TRAINER
1	30 Jul	NewAb	RAHIIB	M.C. Pipe
2	1 Aug	NewAb	BENISA RYDER	M.C. Pipe
3	3 Aug	Devon	BIG PADDY TOM	M.C. Pipe
4	3 Aug	Devon	CELCIUS	M.C. Pipe
5	4 Aug	Devon	STAR OF KUWAIT	M.C. Pipe
6	6 Aug	Sthwl	MY CUP OF TEA	M.C. Pipe
7	10 Aug	Fontw	RULING DYNASTY	R.J. O'Sullivan
8	11 Aug	NewAb	MAINTOWN	M.C. Pipe
9	11 Aug	NewAb	BIG PADDY TOM	M.C. Pipe
10	11 Aug	NewAb	HI-HANNAH	M.C. Pipe
11	11 Aug	NewAb	AFRICAN STAR	M.C. Pipe
12	12 Aug	Devon	BRILLIANT FUTURE	M.C. Pipe
13	12 Aug	Devon	CELCIUS	M.C. Pipe
14	12 Aug	Devon	PERTEMPS NETWORK	M.C. Pipe
15	15 Aug	Worcs	MY CUP OF TEA	M.C. Pipe
16	24 Aug	Devon	PERTEMPS NETWORK	M.C. Pipe
17	24 Aug	Devon	LIADETT (USA)	M.C. Pipe
18	24 Aug	Devon	CHALK PIT	C.P.E. Brooks
19	26 Aug	Bangr	HI-HANNAH	M.C. Pipe
20	29 Aug	NewAb	AFFORD	M.C. Pipe
21	29 Aug	NewAb	AFRICAN STAR	M.C. Pipe
22	29 Aug	NewAb	MY CUP OF TEA	M.C. Pipe
23	31 Aug	NewAb	PERTEMPS NETWORK	M.C. Pipe
24	2 Sep	Hford	CHALK PIT	C.P.E. Brooks
25	3 Sep	Strfd	BRILLIANT FUTURE	M.C. Pipe
26	7 Sep	Fontw	THAT THERE	M.C. Pipe
27	7 Sep	Fontw	LIADETT (USA)	M.C. Pipe
28	8 Sep	NewAb	CHIROPODIST	M.C. Pipe
29	8 Sep	NewAb	AFRICAN STAR	M.C. Pipe
30	8 Sep	NewAb	MY CUP OF TEA	M.C. Pipe
31	9 Sep	NewAb	DICK'S FOLLY	M.C. Pipe
32	17 Sep	Warwk	HIGH KNOWL	M.C. Pipe
33	21 Sep	Devon	INSULAR	I.A. Balding
34	26 Sep	Fontw	CELCIUS	M.C. Pipe
35	26 Sep	Fontw	HI-HANNAH	M.C. Pipe
36	28 Sep	Ludlw	CHIROPODIST	M.C. Pipe
37	5 Oct	Chelt	MY CUP OF TEA	M.C. Pipe
38	5 Oct	Chelt	LIADETT (USA)	M.C. Pipe
39	6 Oct	Chelt	CHALK PIT	C.P.E. Brooks
40	7 Oct	Worcs	CELCIUS	M.C. Pipe
41	8 Oct	Worcs	PARLEZVOUSFRANCAIS	M.C. Pipe

42	11 Oct	NewAb	CHIROPODIST	M.C. Pipe
43	11 Oct	NewAb	TARQOGAN'S BEST	M.C. Pipe
44	12 Oct	Plump	SAYFAR'S LAD	M.C. Pipe
45	13 Oct	Wcntn	AFFORD	M.C. Pipe
46	19 Oct	Chelt	LIADETT (USA)	M.C. Pipe
47	19 Oct	Chelt	MY CUP OF TEA	M.C. Pipe
48	22 Oct	Strfd	ESPY	C.P.E. Brooks
49	24 Oct	Fknhm	WOLFHANGAR	C.P.E. Brooks
50	27 Oct	Wcntn	PHAROAH'S LAEN	M.C. Pipe
51	28 Oct	Devon	THAT THERE	M.C. Pipe
52	29 Oct	Ascot	AFFORD	M.C. Pipe
53	29 Oct	Ascot	BAJAN SUNSHINE	C.P.E. Brooks
54	3 Nov	Kmptn	CANFORD PALM	C.P.E. Brooks
55	4 Nov	Bangr	AFFORD	M.C. Pipe
56	5 Nov	Chpsw	BRUTON STREET	C.P.E. Brooks
57	8 Nov	Devon	SAYFAR'S LAD	M.C. Pipe
58	8 Nov	Devon	FIDDLERS THREE	T.A. Forster
59	8 Nov	Devon	THAT THERE	M.C. Pipe
60	9 Nov	Nbury	DONALD DAVIES	N.A. Twiston-Davies
61	9 Nov	Nbury	WOLFHANGAR	C.P.E. Brooks
62	9 Nov	Nbury	SPRINGHOLM	D. Nicholson
63	11 Nov	MarRn	LAVROSKY (USA)	M.C. Pipe
64	11 Nov	MarRn	BLUE RAINBOW	M.C. Pipe
65	12 Nov	Chelt	PEGWELL BAY	T.A. Forster
66	12 Nov	Chelt	RUN AND SKIP	J.L. Spearing
67	12 Nov	Chelt	LIADETT (USA)	M.C. Pipe
68	14 Nov	Wolv	SWING TO STEEL	M.C. Pipe
69	16 Nov	Kmptn	PENALTY DOUBLE	C.P.E. Brooks
70	16 Nov	Kmptn	ADMIRALS ALL	C.P.E. Brooks
71	17 Nov	Taunt	BLUE RAINBOW	M.C. Pipe
72	17 Nov	Taunt	GOLDEN GLITTER	M.C. Pipe
73	18 Nov	Ascot	MAN ON THE LINE	R. Akehurst
74	18 Nov	Ascot	SABIN DU LOIR (FR)	M.C. Pipe
75	21 Nov	Leicr	CELTIC SHOT	C.P.E. Brooks
76	23 Nov	Hdock	JABRUT	M.C. Pipe
77	23 Nov	Hdock	TARQOGAN'S BEST	M.C. Pipe
78	23 Nov	Hdock	BEAU RANGER	M.C. Pipe
79	24 Nov	Hdock	ENEMY ACTION	M.C. Pipe
80	24 Nov	Hdock	RUN AND SKIP	J.L. Spearing
81	25 Nov	Nbury	PHAROAH'S LAEN	M.C. Pipe
82	25 Nov	Nbury	BARNBROOK AGAIN	D.R.C. Elsworth
83	26 Nov	Nbury	STRANDS OF GOLD	M.C. Pipe
84	29 Nov	NewAb	BONANZA BOY	M.C. Pipe
85	30 Nov	Hford	GO WEST	M.C. Pipe
86	30 Nov	Hford	SUNWOOD	M.C. Pipe
87	30 Nov	Hford	SONDRIO	M.C. Pipe

88	2 Dec	Sand	MAN ON THE LINE	R. Akehurst
89	7 Dec	Huntg	FU'S LADY	M.C. Pipe
90	7 Dec	Huntg	ESPY	C.P.E. Brooks
91	8 Dec	Taunt	SUNWOOD	M.C. Pipe
92	9 Dec	Chelt	ENEMY ACTION	M.C. Pipe
93	12 Dec	Warwk	DEEP MOMENT	Mrs M. Rimell
94	14 Dec	Hdock	SONDRIO	M.C. Pipe
95	14 Dec	Hdock	RUSCH DE FARGES (FR)	M.C. Pipe
96	14 Dec	Hdock	PHAROAH'S LAEN	M.C. Pipe
97	15 Dec	Hdock	STEPASIDE LORD (USA)	M.C. Pipe
98	15 Dec	Hdock	VOYAGE SANS RETOUR (FR)	M.C. Pipe
99	15 Dec	Hdock	FU'S LADY	M.C. Pipe
100	20 Dec	Ludlw	SAYFAR'S LAD	M.C. Pipe
101	20 Dec	Ludlw	SWING TO STEEL	M.C. Pipe
102	20 Dec	Ludlw	CROWECOPPER	B. Preece
103	26 Dec	NewAb	SAYFAR'S LAD	M.C. Pipe
104	26 Dec	NewAb	SABIN DU LOIR (FR)	M.C. Pipe
105	27 Dec	Chpsw	ENEMY ACTION	M.C. Pipe
106	27 Dec	Chpsw	BONANZA BOY	M.C. Pipe
107	27 Dec	Chpsw	FU'S LADY	M.C. Pipe
108	27 Dec	Chpsw	ELEGANT ISLE	M.C. Pipe
109	29 Dec	Taunt	MARETH LINE	M.C. Pipe
110	29 Dec	Taunt	DELKUSHA	M.C. Pipe
111	30 Dec	Nbury	BAIES	C.P.E. Brooks
112	31 Dec	Nbury	BATTLE KING	C.P.E. Brooks
113	5 Jan	Lingf	JUVEN LIGHT (FR)	R. Akehurst
114	5 Jan	Lingf	HONEST WORD	M.C. Pipe
115	6 Jan	Hdock	SILVER ACE	M.C. Pipe
116	7 Jan	Hdock	ROLLING BALL (FR)	M.C. Pipe
117	7 Jan	Hdock	MARETH LINE	M.C. Pipe
118	7 Jan	Hdock	STOCKSIGN (USA)	B.L. Key
119	9 Jan	Wolv	ELEGANT ISLE	M.C. Pipe
120	9 Jan	Wolv	BATTALION (USA)	C.P.E. Brooks
121	9 Jan	Wolv	BALUCHI	B. Preece
122	10 Jan	NewAb	OUT OF THE GLOOM	M.C. Pipe
123	10 Jan	NewAb	RUSCH DE FARGES (FR)	M.C. Pipe
124	10 Jan	NewAb	MIGHT MOVE	M.C. Pipe
125	11 Jan	Plump	ROSCOE HARVEY	C.P.E. Brooks
126	13 Jan	Ascot	SABIN DU LOIR (FR)	M.C. Pipe
127	14 Jan	Ascot	PERTEMPS NETWORK	M.C. Pipe
128	14 Jan	Ascot	SONDRIO	M.C. Pipe
129	17 Jan	Worcs	FETCHAM PARK	M.C. Pipe
130	17 Jan	Worcs	CELTIC FLIGHT	Mrs M. Rimell
131	18 Jan	Ludlw	KINGS RANK	M.C. Pipe
132	19 Jan	Lingf	JUVEN LIGHT (FR)	R. Akehurst
133	19 Jan	Lingf	HONEST WORD	M.C. Pipe

134	20 Jan	Kmptn	BATTALION (USA)	C.P.E. Brooks
135	21 Jan	Hdock	OUT OF THE GLOOM	M.C. Pipe
136	21 Jan	Hdock	BRUTON STREET	C.P.E. Brooks
137	24 Jan	Chpsw	CANFORD PALM	C.P.E. Brooks
138	24 Jan	Chpsw	ELVERCONE	A.J. Wilson
139	25 Jan	Wolv	BALUCHI	B. Preece
140	25 Jan	Wolv	PROTECTION	Andrew Turnell
141	26 Jan	Taunt	LE CYGNE	M.C. Pipe
142	27 Jan	Wcntn	PUKKA MAJOR (USA)	T. Thomson Jones
143	31 Jan	Leicr	TEL-ECHO	M.C. Pipe
144	31 Jan	Leicr	BALUCHI	B. Preece
145	31 Jan	Leicr	CELCIUS	M.C. Pipe
146	1 Feb	Hford	ADMIRALS ALL	C.P.E. Brooks
147	2 Feb	Lingf	WINGSPAN (USA)	M.C. Pipe
148	6 Feb	Fontw	DELKUSHA	M.C. Pipe
149	6 Feb	Fontw	BATTALION (USA)	C.P.E. Brooks
150	7 Feb	Warwk	ANTI MATTER	M.C. Pipe
151	7 Feb	Warwk	PERTEMPS NETWORK	M.C. Pipe
152	8 Feb	Ascot	SABIN DU LOIR (FR)	M.C. Pipe
153	10 Feb	Nbury	JUVEN LIGHT (FR)	R. Akehurst
154	11 Feb	Nbury	ADMIRALS ALL	C.P.E. Brooks
155	13 Feb	Nttm	THE GAELCHARN	C.P.E. Brooks
156	14 Feb	NewAb	WINGSPAN (USA)	M.C. Pipe
157	14 Feb	NewAb	LET HIM BY	M.C. Pipe
158	14 Feb	NewAb	AVIONNE	M.C. Pipe
159	15 Feb	Worcs	BALUCHI	B. Preece
160	15 Feb	Worcs	SAYFAR'S LAD	M.C. Pipe
161	16 Feb	Leicr	AU BON	M.C. Pipe
162	18 Feb	Nttm	PHOENIX GOLD	J.G. FitzGerald
163	20 Feb	Fontw	LET HIM BY	M.C. Pipe
164	22 Feb	Warwk	SAYFAR'S LAD	M.C. Pipe
165	22 Feb	Warwk	PHAROAH'S LAEN	M.C. Pipe
166	22 Feb	Warwk	TRAVEL MYSTERY	M.C. Pipe
167	23 Feb	Folks	GO WEST	M.C. Pipe
168	25 Feb	Kmptn	BONANZA BOY	M.C. Pipe
169	28 Feb	Nttm	LE CYGNE	M.C. Pipe
170	1 Mar	Worcs	BEAU RANGER	M.C. Pipe
171	2 Mar	Lingf	KUMAKAS NEPHEW	M.C. Pipe
172	4 Mar	Hford	SILVER ACE	M.C. Pipe
173	4 Mar	Hford	GO WEST	M.C. Pipe
174	4 Mar	Nbury	ADMIRALS ALL	C.P.E. Brooks
175	4 Mar	Nbury	PERTEMPS NETWORK	M.C. Pipe
176	11 Mar	Chpsw	FETCHAM PARK	M.C. Pipe
177	11 Mar	Sand	TRAVEL MYSTERY	M.C. Pipe
178	14 Mar	Chelt	PUKKA MAJOR (USA)	T. Thomson Jones
179	17 Mar	Wolv	LE CYGNE	M.C. Pipe

180	17 Mar	Wolv	MITHRAS	B. Preece
181	18 Mar	Lingf	SILVER ACE	M.C. Pipe
182	22 Mar	Worcs	TEMPLE REEF	M.C. Pipe
183	22 Mar	Worcs	FANDANGO BOY	M.C. Pipe
184	22 Mar	Worcs	CELCIUS	M.C. Pipe
185	23 Mar	Taunt	ANTI MATTER	M.C. Pipe
186	27 Mar	Chpsw	CELTIC SHOT	C.P.E. Brooks
187	27 Mar	Chpsw	GO WEST	M.C. Pipe
188	27 Mar	Chpsw	HILARION (FR)	J.A.C. Edwards
189	28 Mar	Chpsw	OLD KILPATRICK	M.C. Pipe
190	29 Mar	Worcs	ELVERCONE	A.J. Wilson
191	13 Apr	Ludlw	JUST ROSE	M.C. Pipe
192	15 Apr	Bangr	AU BON	M.C. Pipe
193	15 Apr	Bangr	WINGSPAN (USA)	M.C. Pipe
194	18 Apr	Devon	OLD KILPATRICK	M.C. Pipe
195	20 Apr	Chelt	VOYAGE SANS RETOUR (FR)	M.C. Pipe
196	22 Apr	Uttox	HIGH BID	M.C. Pipe
197	24 Apr	Sthwl	AVIONNE	M.C. Pipe
198	27 Apr	Towcr	OLD KILPATRICK	M.C. Pipe
199	27 Apr	Towcr	CANFORD PALM	C.P.E. Brooks
200	27 Apr	Towcr	GAY MOORE	M.H. Robinson